FORAGE & FEAST

FORAGE & FEAST

Chrissy Tracey

Recipes for Bringing Mushrooms & Wild Plants to Your Table

Photographs by
Chrissy Tracey &
Natalie Black

TEN SPEED PRESS
California | New York

To all the adults who forever want to play in the mud, this one's for you.

CONTENTS

WELCOME, SUMMER 88

INTRODUCTION

"Come on, the sun is up! Let's go outside after breakfast!"
I exclaimed to my next-door neighbor Shannon as the cord of the house phone curled around my little hands. I smashed down the phone and rushed to get ready, looking in the mirror to pat down my afro before going to see what my parents were cooking.

My dad stood in the kitchen in his slippers and socks, sweatpants, and a rolled-up windbreaker over a cut-off T-shirt, surrounded by the scent of oatmeal. "Come eat!" he said in his thick Jamaican accent. Growing up, I loved when my dad made my oatmeal for me—always with brown sugar and berries. I would stand by his side as he cooked, and persuade him to add more sugar. People often have cornmeal- or oatmeal-based porridge for breakfast in Jamaica, and that joyful morning ritual was one of the many ways my parents effortlessly integrated our family heritage into my childhood.

I was five when I realized that I wanted to spend my days exploring nature. From sunrise to sunset, no one could find me. Shannon, who loved being outdoors as much as I did, would be waiting for me before I finished my last spoonful of oatmeal. After breakfast, we would embark on one of our adventures, spending the day in the untrodden woods of Cheshire, Connecticut, admiring and connecting with nature. These innocent mornings were filled with the scent of pine trees, skunk cabbages, and morning dew.

It was during these magical days that I discovered my first forageable foods. "Look, Mom!" I cried out breathlessly. "Wild garlic! It smells so good! Can I eat it? I'm pretty sure it's garlic. It smells like garlic. It looks like garlic!" Every spring I feel the very same thrill of discovery, as though it's my first day exploring the woods. I remember the taste of juicy wineberries, a deliciously sweet variety of raspberry that grew at the edge of the woods by my childhood home. They were my absolute favorite. I can still feel the thorns pricking my little fingers while I searched for the juiciest, most plump berries. I ate them until my heart was content.

At the end of every summer, when wild grapes grew in, I forced myself to taste the fruit, which made my mouth pucker with each bite. Even though they were sour, just knowing that they were edible was reason enough for me to try them. The undeniable curiosity to explore, find, and eat wild foods has stayed with me all my life, and what began as playful childhood adventures evolved into a lifelong passion for foraged cooking. The reward of taking a mushroom home for flavor and sustenance still overwhelms my brain with a satisfying rush of dopamine.

Foraging is a deeply sensory activity. It often begins with seeing a plant or mushroom, followed by smelling, touching, and, finally, tasting it. When you find something new, you bring it home, observe it, and, once you have positively identified it, eat it. I think that is why I have such a deep love and respect for foraging. You become one with the ingredient before you even taste it, and you gain a closer relationship with your food. I had one of my first experiences with cooking when I was about twelve years old. Our new next-door neighbors, a couple from Argentina, had a daughter, Denise, who was about my age, and we quickly became friends. I loved watching her mother, Sabrina, cook effortlessly while the Spanish pop ballad "Soy Rebelde," by Jeannette, played in the background. One day, I asked if I could cook with her. We made fresh cracked–black pepper pasta, carrot cake (my favorite), and empanadas. Sabrina always encouraged and nurtured my exploratory spirit, and because of her lessons, I quickly decided that the kitchen was a space I wanted to be in forever.

In high school, I took a business class in which I created a proposal for a dream venture centered around making vegetarian and vegan food accessible, affordable, and delicious. My parents had raised their seven kids on a vegetarian diet when plant-based food was nowhere near as widely available as it is today. I wanted to fix the problems that I faced as the girl who always had to get fries and a salad because there were no other vegetarian options. I brought that business plan to life in my second year of college, when I started my own catering company, Chrissy's. While working a full-time tech job, I committed to keeping my food career foremost in my mind. The one person who always believed in and encouraged me was my dad. He worked hard to realize every dream he ever had and, together with my mother, nurtured that same work ethic in me. They accomplished everything they wanted to do in life, despite starting with very little, and they inspire me daily.

In 2019, I embarked on my first professional restaurant experience in New Haven, Connecticut—the pizza capital of the world. Thanks to the success of my catering business, I was hired at a well-known pizza joint, Da Legna at Nolo. I was in charge of managing the large, imported wood-fired pizza ovens, and, as the only woman working in the kitchen, I was known as "the pizza girl." I always found ways to "veganize" the classic pies, and the highlight of my job was my Meatless Monday program. On those days, in addition to making a line of vegan pizzas with inspired cheese alternatives, I was able to introduce the community to inventive plant-based main plates and desserts. The concept quickly took off, and omnivores would line up, much to my surprise, asking when the next event was. That's the moment I realized I was on to something big and took the leap to center my entire life around cooking. I expanded my catering business, and, soon after, quit my day job. Chrissy's was a success. And yet it felt like something was missing. I found myself seeking the adventurous, childlike spirit that first connected me with food. I wanted to explore and incorporate wild, unique vegetables in ways that would surprise and delight my clients. I knew I needed to get back into nature.

My return to the wild began in 2019 with regular hikes and finding new sites that brought me joy. On one expedition in Wolcott, Connecticut, where I enjoyed walking, I had a revelation. I slowed down and stopped chasing the views at the top, taking time to smell the spruce pines. I walked through old forest, admiring the beauty of the wild trillium flowers that grew by the lake. At the edge of the water, I stumbled upon a patch of wild garlic, which I loved so much as a child. I picked a chive, and pure joy came flooding back as I nibbled on it. It is and always has been the wild garlic that inspires me. At that moment, I knew what I had to do: It was time for me to explore the unknown and master uncharted territories.

Foraging is the closest thing I've found to treasure hunting, and personally, the treasures I find in the woods are more precious than gold. My relationship to foraging intensified and reignited my passion for learning. The practice provides a lot of space for growth, discovery, and innovation. For me, it feels ancestrally connective, deeply rooted in stories and experiences I have never known but are within me. I shouldn't have been so surprised by my fascination with wild ingredients. As a first-generation Jamaican American, foraging is in my blood. I was sixteen years old the first time I went to Jamaica. I remember it being a big deal for my parents, who came to the United States to live the American dream. It was a moment where their eyes said "we made it" without them saying anything at all. They couldn't wait for the day where our family of nine ventured to their homeland and experienced a bit of what life was like through their eyes. Upon our arrival, Grandma Hazel, eager to share a meal with us, went straight outside to harvest native fruits and veggies that grew wild in her backyard. I was immediately captivated by the way she lived—a lifestyle once necessary for the original inhabitants of the country.

In the 1800s, the Maroon people, a group of Africans who escaped slavery, hid away in the mountainous regions of Jamaica. They survived, in part, by foraging from the abundant edible wild plants on the ancient Caribbean island, including plantains, maize, yams, and a variety of root vegetables. They also hunted wild animals. Most of the communities formed in inaccessible areas—unpopulated, yet dense with vegetation. To this day, foraging and preserving native plants are important tools for combating food insecurity. Jamaica might be an impoverished country, but it is rich in biodiversity.

Foraging has come to mean so much more to me since I realized how connected it is to my Jamaican heritage. Little did I know when I first started exploring the woods that it would become a major inspiration for my culinary career. Professionally I'm a vegan chef, but I often think of myself as more than that: I'm a forager and an innovator. I am constantly attempting to find new ways of making plant-based foods fun, exciting, and accessible. I often incorporate foraged foods into the work I do today, whether I'm catering, cooking as a private chef or at a special event, or entertaining friends.

Forage & Feast will help you create beautifully plated meals with unique garnishes, prepared with gorgeous foraged ingredients. It is meant to inspire adventures in the forest and kitchen, and feed your creative spirit. I hope this book inspires you to do something new— like learning a new cooking technique, identifying a plant for the first time, or, at the very least, taking the time to slow down and enjoy the little things in life. At first, the art of foraging can seem otherworldly and even a little bit scary. But this book will help equip you with the basic knowledge necessary to successfully cook with wild foraged edibles. We'll explore the world of plants and fungi throughout the four seasons and reframe the way we think about seasonal eating. Join me on a riveting culinary adventure filled with mystery, great food, and lots of fun.

Come on, the sun is up! Let's go outside!

FORAGING 101

Online communities are essential. They help you build deep, meaningful relationships with like-minded individuals. And in the case of foraging, they provide ways to learn hands-on and as a team, rather than on your own. My foraging community is incredible, and I am eternally grateful for the knowledge I have gained from those with whom I've crossed paths, both virtually and in person. I sought the advice of my foraging mentors and acquaintances to come up with the following tips and best practices. You will find additional resources, including helpful books and apps, at the back of this book.

1. **Check the foraging rules in your state and for each park or nature preserve you plan to visit.** Every state has different rules about foraging. Some, such as California, simply don't allow it unless it is on your own property. Others, such as Connecticut, permit foraging on specific nature preserves, with rules to protect endangered species or rehabilitate the environment. Still others, like Vermont, have freedom to roam laws, which allow you to walk openly on anyone's land, unless explicitly prohibited. Regardless of the state laws, if you are on private property, make sure you have permission from the landowners before you harvest. You don't want to get in trouble for harvesting in a space in which you aren't welcome to forage. Checking the local laws is imperative for a great, safe experience without any problems. Typically rules are posted on the entrance signs to parks. And you can find your state's laws on the state's government website. Alternatively, you can call the department of environmental protection to find out more information.

2. **Learn the local trees.** Once you can successfully identify the trees in your area, you'll more easily find the wild plants and mushrooms that live in their vicinity, resulting in more successful foraging adventures. The US Environmental Protection Agency provides state listings of the native trees and shrubs that grow in your area, so use them to learn your chances of finding certain mushrooms or plants. The National Audubon Society publishes a field guide to North American trees, which is a great resource for learning how to identify them. I live in the

northeastern United States, and if you do too, I'd recommend *A Beginner's Guide to Recognizing Trees of the Northeast* by Mark Mikolas (2017).

3. **Get to know a few wooded trails.** You can find mushrooms in *every* forest, so focus on areas near you. Choose three diverse woods large enough to walk in for a minimum of twenty minutes. Visit each spot you find in those woods three times a week. Start on a trail and learn the area well; it's easy to get turned around and lost. Once you get comfortable, use the trail as the center of the circle and, when you leave the trail, keep your radius manageable so that you don't get disoriented. Use a compass. With this strategy, your chances of foraging success will be much higher.

4. **Be courteous.** If someone brings you to their foraging location, always return to that place *with* them. This is nonnegotiable. Never tell anyone else about that site without the express permission of the person who showed it to you. It's bad karma. It took time, effort, and work for them to find that place. No one wants the magical area of wild edibles that they rely on every year to become overharvested. Sadly, this happens a lot, and foragers are known to be secretive because of this. Never give away one of your spots unless you're alright with the possibility that it might be shared with people you don't know.

5. **Slow down and think before you pick.** Don't be overly confident in your ability to identify a plant or mushroom species at first look. To properly identify it, you need to learn and be able to confidently ID all of its toxic lookalikes. It's too easy to mistake a toxic plant or mushroom for an edible one, especially for a novice. The practice of foraging requires study and close attention to detail, just like any other skill. You must work at it and constantly refine your skill. Err on the side of caution and assume that you are not always right. This may sound overwhelming, but you never want a foraging experience to be your last.

6. **If you aren't 100 percent sure about a mushroom you picked, consult an experienced forager.** This is where the power of community is invaluable. I usually feel quite confident trusting foragers who have their certification (which is not mandatory to be a great forager, but it does mean they've been properly educated), or someone who has years of experience. I still often seek the advice of more experienced foragers than myself, because multiple educated opinions are better than just my own. Consult your community as much as possible, in addition to identifying plants and mushrooms with the use of a field guide.

Wild carrots (*Daucus carota*). They are often referred to as "Queen Anne's lace" due to their delicate flowers that resemble lace patterns.

7. **ALWAYS cook the mushrooms you forage before you eat them.** While there are a few raw-edible species, they are rare, so it is best to get in the habit of cooking all mushrooms to minimize risk.

8. **Don't be greedy.** Take what you need and leave the rest. Make sure to leave some for the creatures to eat. Many deer, slugs, and other animals thrive on the same mushrooms and plant species that humans enjoy. Consider what you will do with the wild foods that you've found. How will you preserve them? If this is your first time properly inspecting or identifying a plant or mushroom, just take one or two to study at home. You can never be too sure about your findings, so do not start out your foraging journey by overharvesting.

9. **Leave no trace.** This means leaving the forest undisturbed, as though you were never there. Out of respect for nature and consideration for others who may come down the path after you, don't kick mushrooms or knock them over for fun. Bring an extra bag with you to pick up trash when you go out foraging. If you can pick up a mushroom or a plant to bring home, you can pick up trash too. Give back to Mother Nature and her forests. It's the least we can do.

10. **Always bring a buddy.** Foraging with others means you will have the benefit of their opinions when identifying a plant or mushroom, and it is also a safer way to explore. If you can, always forage with another person or in a small group. It ends up being a lot of fun, even if you don't find what you are looking for!

11. **To ensure your safety, be prepared.** Bring ample water and snacks. You never want to run out of water while in the woods, and you want snacks on hand so that you don't lose steam during your trek. While foraging, it's a good idea to wear bright colors, especially orange, as you never know when you are sharing the area with hunters. Wearing orange will help ensure you aren't mistaken for prey. It's easy to get lost in the woods, especially if you go off trail. You may end up in the dark, so carrying a flashlight is always smart. Using a compass to help you stay on track and noting the coordinates of where you entered the woods to begin with are also good ideas. A whistle can help others find you if you get lost. Technology is also great when we use it to our benefit. Always let a few people know your whereabouts, and share your location on your smartphone. That way, should anything happen to you, you'll be easier to find. Charge your phone completely before you head out and use it sparingly to preserve your battery. If you have an iPhone, you may also want to keep an Apple AirTag on you. Apple AirTags are small tracking devices that send out a secure Bluetooth signal that can be detected by other Apple device owners in the Find My

network, which uses Bluetooth wireless technology to detect the approximate location of Apple devices or items and report back to their owners. It is anonymous and encrypted, so your privacy is protected, but you can still be findable by others who may be exploring nearby.

12. **Be wary of bears and other animals.** Bears often leave you alone, but not always. If you see a bear cub, keep moving, because its mama will be nearby. Mama bears can get quite aggressive to protect their young. In general, when you see a bear, try to keep calm and move on. If they start to show signs of aggression—usually they'll stare, protrude their lower lip, and flatten their ears, or huff and swat the ground—try your best to appear big, by raising your arms above your shoulders and waving them around, and make a lot of loud noises. Carry bear spray with you, as it tends to work as a deterrent for many potentially dangerous animals. A general rule of thumb is to try to be noisy while in the woods. It is usually enough to keep unwanted wildlife away while you wander about. Remember, we are in their territory, not the other way around.

13. **Coming back empty-handed from a forage is only a failure if you haven't learned anything.** Foraging is about the adventure. It's about smelling the spruce pine, the flowers, and the fungi. It's about getting outside and moving your body. It's more than just the harvest, and very much about enjoying nature and learning to love and appreciate it more deeply with each exploration. It's a journey.

14. **Hang out and learn from others who know more than you, and don't be afraid of being corrected.** This is perhaps the most important tip. You must be humble when learning how to forage. It's not cool to be cocky or think you are always right. Learn to be vulnerable. Go in with the mindset that everyone is just trying to help you and that concern for your safety is at the forefront of everyone's mind. Positive intent goes a long way.

Identifying fungi can be tricky, and one of the simplest ways to avoid misidentification is by making a spore print. Microscopic spores are released from fungi for reproduction and contain all the necessary material to form a new fungus. The fruiting bodies of fungi are called mushrooms, and mushrooms are responsible for releasing spores. Mushrooms come in many shapes and forms, so it's important to understand what you are identifying using the following traits before doing a spore print, so you can complete the task correctly.

Color. Mushrooms come in a variety of colors, and one species may come in multiple hues. Color is one of the defining characteristics of mushrooms, so know what to look for and keep a keen eye out in the field when foraging.

Habitat. Unlike plants, some mushrooms have a symbiotic relationship with a particular tree species. You'll want to know what types of trees to look for in mixed forests while out foraging. An ability to identify tree species is crucial for learning how to forage.

Shape. Mushrooms vary in shape, from their caps to their stems. For example, black trumpet mushrooms quite literally have a trumpetlike shape, making it one of the key identifiers of the species. Some mushrooms, such as chicken of the woods, do not have "true" caps. Rather, what would typically be called a cap is referred to as the "upper surface."

Size. Mushrooms vary in size and structure, so it is important to understand the dimensions of each mushroom you are trying to identify.

Staining. Some mushrooms stain, or bleed, different colors when the surface is touched or cut by a knife. These color changes are very important and can help you to identify whether a mushroom you've found is poisonous.

Underside. Underneath the mushroom caps, a variety of features, such as gills or pores and the presence of a veil, may help you identify to which family it belongs.

WAYS TO IDENTIFY MUSHROOMS & OTHER FUNGI

Yellow fly agaric
(*Amanita muscaria var. guessowii*)

Dune brittlestem (*Psathyrella ammophila*)

Hedgehog mushroom
(*Hydnum repandum*)

Bicolor bolete (*Baorangia bicolor*)

Of course, there are other ways to identify mushrooms, but for me, these are among the most important. To learn more about what to look for, join a local mycology association and get hands-on experience with experts in the field.

SPORE PRINTING

Spore printing is a method used in mycology to obtain a pattern of spores from the cap of a mushroom or another fungus by placing it on a piece of paper or glass. The spores are released overnight, forming a distinctive configuration, which can be used to identify the species. This technique is commonly used in scientific research and in identifying edible mushrooms.

It's best to do a spore print when a mushroom is fresh, immediately after returning from the field. Cut off the stem and place the cap, gills down, on a white piece of paper, aluminum foil, or glass. Spritz the top of the cap with water, cover with a paper cup or drinking glass, and leave for up to 24 hours. If a mushroom is fresh and damp, sometimes you can get a confirmed spore print in as little as 2 hours.

Mushrooms with Gills. Some mushrooms have gills, a ribbed underside beneath the cap, which vary in color, shape, and size depending on the species.

Mushrooms with Pores. Some mushrooms have pores that reside underneath their caps. They look like little holes but are actually the ends of tubes inside the cap, which release spores, giving the underside a spongy appearance.

Other Fungi Forms. Some mushrooms and other fungi, such as morels and lobster fungi, have unusual shapes. To take a spore print, you'll have to first study them and determine from where the spores are released. Luckily, some mushrooms will spore in a way that is more visible to the human eye. For example, scarlet cup fungi have a cap that is inverted like a cup, and the spores are released upward in little clouds that are discernible when the light hits them. This allows you to see where the spores are released in the field and will help you determine mushroom placement when obtaining a spore print. In nature, mushroom spores can resemble tiny dust particles, as they are typically small and light enough to be carried by the wind. Experiment with placing the specimen in different positions until you get a proper spore print, and record the process.

What you wear in the woods is important, as ticks tend to be abundant. Dressing in shorts to stay cool and comfortable is not worth the risk of getting Lyme disease, Rocky Mountain Spotted Fever, or babesiosis from a tick bite. I have seen the effects of Lyme disease impact so many people in my life, and it can be devastating. Of course, that isn't the only reason to be cautious about your clothing. The woods contain other trials, such as poison ivy and thorny brambles.

WHAT TO WEAR IN THE WOODS

1. **Proper footwear.** In the woods, you'll want to be as comfortable as possible, as it is easy to spend hours on a foraging adventure. You'll often encounter varying terrain, from rocky hills to wetlands, so it's important to be prepared for the environment in which you'll be foraging. I recommend water-resistant hiking boots with good traction, or sturdy, ankle-high, waterproof sneakers. I tend to pair my hiking boots with long wool socks to protect my ankles and shins.

2. **Comfortable clothing is a must.** When you're out in the woods, wear loose, comfortable clothing that allows you to move freely. Consider the season and layer as you see fit. I always suggest wearing a linen or cotton-blend jumpsuit with full sleeves and long pants, leggings, or comfortable leisure wear that covers your legs and arms completely. During the summer, go for white or lighter colors so that you can avoid overheating. If you are in vast, open woods, it's okay to remove layers; just be cautious when going into dense thickets.

3. **Wear a bright-orange jacket or pinny.** Check your local hunting laws, as during certain months of the year, foragers must share the woods with hunters. This poses serious danger. You do not want a hunter to mistake you for game. The easiest way to announce your presence is to wear bright colors when you go out in the woods. I also wear a bright-orange beanie.

MY FAVORITE FORAGING TOOLS

Experienced foragers keep tool kits with everything they could possibly need in the woods. Here, I have compiled a list of some of my favorite foraging equipment, which I think a new forager should have on hand.

Foraging Basket, Backpack, or Mesh Bag. A great wicker or straw foraging basket or backpack is essential. I prefer something that is easy to carry around and doesn't get in my way while I'm moving about in the woods. Check your local Goodwill for wicker gathering baskets; they usually have an inexpensive selection! Recommended: The Primary Boom mesh backpack from Glob. This backpack is my favorite, as there are small holes from top to bottom, which allow mushroom spores to drop and spread easily after being harvested. How cool is that! I also like the Foraging Bag from Barebones, which is stylish and highly functional. It allows you to store a good volume of wild edibles, and it has a mesh bottom and a bucket-style opening. It's great for foraging plants and fungi. Another suggestion is the Herschel Supply Co. Survey Backpack, which is weather resistant.

Foraging Knife. Having a great foraging knife will vastly improve your experience. I always have a pocketknife with me, as well as a hooked-blade knife. The arched foraging knife is great for harvesting thick, dense fungi, while a pocketknife is excellent for harvesting more fragile plants and mushrooms. Recommended: Double L pocketknife (one blade), from L.L. Bean, and the Victorinox pruning knife (one large blade).

Gardening Gloves. Many plants and shrubs, such as berry brambles and stinging nettle, can make harvesting difficult. A good pair of gardening gloves is imperative, so that you can easily handle any plant species while keeping your hands safe from cuts. Recommended: Barebones leather work gloves and Pine Tree Tools bamboo gardening gloves.

Kitchen Shears. Kitchen shears go a long way. My advice is to always have a pair on you for harvesting tender greens and tougher stemmed plants. Recommended: Ergo Chef kitchen shears. I particularly like these shears because they come apart for easy cleaning. They are also heavy-duty and can cut through just about anything. I use them to trim flowers, mint, nettles, and more.

Vegetable Brush. Some wild foods are full of dirt and debris, especially fungi. A good vegetable brush can help you clean them with ease. Recommended: The vegetable brush from OXO.

Many of the recipes in this book call for sterilized mason jars, also known as canning jars, to store your foraged creations properly and successfully without bacterial growth. When a mason jar and its components are properly sterilized, you can keep shelf-stable jams, preserved mushrooms, and more for up to a year. Knowing how to sterilize safely and effectively is very important, so I'll give you the breakdown on how to do this. It will give you peace of mind.

HOW TO STERILIZE MASON JARS

THINGS TO CONSIDER

- Not every jar labeled "mason jar" is designed to withstand the intense heat of the canning process. Read labels carefully, as you don't want broken glass in your kitchen, resulting in possible injury and the loss of your precious preserved foods.

- Authentic canning jars have a threaded neck and come with screw bands and lids, which are smooth and flat.

- You can purchase mason jars at grocery stores, hardware stores, and general merchandise stores.

- Canning jars are intended for moist environments, not dry heat. Do not attempt to place canning jars in an oven or over an open flame.

- The jars are not designed for sudden temperature changes, and thermal shock can cause them to break. For that reason, place hot jars on a heatproof tray or wooden surface, rather than a stainless-steel one.

- When filling jars, avoid using metal utensils, as a scrape from a different material can cause the glass to break.

- Do not use rusty, dirty, or misshapen lids.

WHAT TO BUY

- **Boiling Water Canner with Lid and Wire Rack.** The pot is large and the rack fits inside. They are used in the boiling-water process for sterilizing and canning. Stainless steel is best.

- **Canning Funnels.** Canning funnels allow you to fill jars more easily, with fewer spills.

- **Jar Lifters.** Lift hot mason jars with these long tongs. You can also use long, rubber-coated, heat-resistant tongs.

- **Nonmetal Spatulas.** Silicone is best, as it's heat-resistant, nonreactive, and more sanitary than wooden utensils.

THE CANNING PROCESS

Foraging demands patience, time, and effort, but sometimes you may hit the jackpot and find an abundance of edible mushrooms and plants. However, like store-bought veggies, these treasures have a short shelf life. To avoid waste and enjoy your bounty year-round, consider canning. It's one of my favorite preservation methods, and I highly recommend it when you have plenty to preserve!

1. Prepare the recipe you are using as directed. The jars and lids will only remain hot for 30 minutes once sterilized, so it is best to have the food ready to go.

2. Wash the jars and lids and bands with hot soapy water, rinse, and drain.

3. Place a rack in the bottom of a boiling water canner, and put the required number of mason jars on the rack. If the jars are 8 ounces or smaller, add water to the jars and canner until it reaches the tops of the jars. If they are larger, add enough water so the jars are two-thirds full and the water in the canner comes two-thirds of the way up the sides of the jars.

4. Cover the canner and bring the water to a simmer over medium heat. When the water registers 180°F on an instant-read thermometer, using a jar lifter, remove the jars from the heat.

5. Meanwhile, place all lids and bands inside a separate small saucepan and cover with water. Place over medium heat and bring the water to 180°F. Using tongs, remove the lids and bands from the heat.

6. Carefully place the prepared food into the hot jars, leaving some headspace between the top of the jar and the top of the food. For pickles, mushrooms, tomatoes, fruits, and condiments, you'll need ½ inch of headspace. For soft spreads and fruit juice, you'll need ¼ inch of headspace.

7. Using a rubber spatula, stir the contents of the jar to release any air bubbles.

8. Using a clean paper towel, wipe the jar rim; this will help the jar seal more effectively. Then, using the tongs, place a hot lid on each jar, being sure that there is no excess water on them, and screw on the bands.

9. Place the jars back on the rack in the hot water–filled canning pot, and bring to a full boil.

10. Turn off the heat, then lift the jars out of the water. Place them upright on a towel or wire rack and allow to cool for up to 24 hours. Store in a cool, dark place for up to 1 year.

You may be new to foraging and apprehensive about cooking with what you find—I don't blame you! It can be intimidating to jump right in. And you may not have access to certain wild foods in your area depending on the climate or season, which is understandable. Here is a list of swaps for the foraged foods featured in the recipes in this book. You can also omit certain ingredients if sourcing them is simply not possible for you, though the dish may not taste the same. There are online markets, such as Fresh & Wild, Foraged, Etsy, and Northwest Wild Foods, that sell a lot of wild goodies when in season. When cooking with foraged items, you've got to get creative!

Beach Plums. You can replace beach plums with red or black plums from the grocery store, although these varieties aren't as tart or nuanced as beach plums.

Chanterelles. You can purchase chanterelles online from one of the select markets noted above. Alternatively, some farmers' market vendors will sell these when they're in season.

Chicken of the Woods. There is no good swap for this, so it's best to look for it online or at your local farmers' market.

Crabapples. Granny Smith apples or any other tart and crisp varietal work as a replacement.

Dandelion. There is no alternative for dandelion flowers; however, the greens are often sold at supermarkets when in season. As an alternative, you can sub arugula, radicchio, or chicory for the leaves.

Fiddlehead Ferns. The best swap for fiddlehead ferns is peas, pea shoots, asparagus, or green beans.

Field Garlic. Garlic and chives are easy swaps.

Garlic Mustard. There isn't an ideal swap for this one, so you must get creative. Try a combination of mustard greens and parsley, mixed with a clove or two of garlic.

Japanese Knotweed. The best swap is rhubarb.

Japanese Wineberries. You can swap wineberries for cultivated raspberries.

King Bolete (Porcini). Many grocery stores sell dried porcini mushrooms. You can also buy them online from Foraged market when in season.

GROCERY STORE SWAPS

Pictured here are shiitake mushrooms being home grown using a method called inoculation.

Lion's Mane. There is no great swap for this mushroom, but you can sometimes find lion's mane, grown by indoor-mushroom cultivators, in specialty grocery stores or in Whole Foods.

Lobster Fungi. There is no great swap for this, but you can try mixing kelp powder with button mushrooms for a similar flavor and hearty texture.

Magnolia Flowers. Ginger is the closest flavor to magnolia that you can find at a grocery store, but it will not quite work for a one-to-one swap due to its lack of floral notes. Play around and mix ginger with edible flowers, like violets, black locust flowers, roses, and marigolds, to get the essence of magnolia flowers.

Maitake. You can find maitake mushrooms at specialty grocery stores, Whole Foods, or directly from cultivators in your area.

Maple. Store-bought maple syrup is often as good as homemade, especially if you are purchasing from local or small-batch producers!

Matsutake. There is no ideal swap for this mushroom, but you can find them online either fresh, when in season, or dried from one of the markets noted previously.

Morel Mushrooms. There is nothing quite like morels, but you can swap out this mushroom for shiitake or oyster mushrooms, which can be found in most grocery stores and wherever there are local producers.

Pawpaws. A one-to-one mix of mango and banana is a good replacement.

Pine Needles. There is nothing quite like pine, but you can always rely on a mix of lemon, lime, and grapefruit to get a similar flavor.

Purslane. You can buy this from most gardening shops, as it is often grown as a household plant!

Ramps. Leeks, spring onions, and shallots can all work as replacements.

Shagbark Hickory. You can swap the nuts for walnuts or pecans, as they taste quite similar.

Staghorn Sumac. You can find the spice dried sumac in many specialty grocery stores, at Arab and Armenian markets, and at Whole Foods.

Stinging Nettle. When in season, you can often find stinging nettle at farmers' markets across the United States. Otherwise, try swapping stinging nettle for a mix of one part mint to ten parts spinach to bring the essence of stinging nettle to a recipe. Or just use spinach.

Sugar Kelp. Use nori sheets instead of sugar kelp if you are unable to harvest it. You'll find nori in many supermarkets as well as in Asian markets.

Wild Blueberries. Cultivated blueberries can be used; they just aren't as sweet or flavorful as the wild ones.

Wild Mint. Store-bought, cultivated mint is a perfect replacement. Alternatively, your local gardening center probably has a few interesting varieties.

Wintergreen. Purchase wintergreen extract from specialty grocers online, or swap with peppermint extract.

01

HELLO, SPRING

The sun was beginning to set. Bold hues of yellow, orange, and red ochre shone through the trees. This was our fourth day of searching for ramps. Neither forest, nor marsh, nor plain had yielded the slightest hint of them. We sniffed the air hoping for even the faintest scent of onion in the passing winds. We were only guided by the words of an old forager, which I'll never forget: I would find ramps "where sandy shores meet nutrient-dense forests." We turned up every rock, root, and piece of greenery we saw. Trout lily! Daylily! But no ramps, although the leaves looked similar to the uncertain eye. There is one thing every forager agrees upon—you'll know it when you find it. Uncertainty was failure.

This was the third nature preserve we had tried. An almost untouched, prehistoric lake, in a quaint town in northeastern Connecticut. Trekking around the lake, we ventured on and off trail through mud and intermittent rain juxtaposed against the setting sun. Eventually, we returned to the path, ready to head home. As we circled back to the trailhead, a beam of sunlight shone upon a patch of greenery. Could it be? As we came closer, we noticed a garlicky, oniony smell permeating the area. What my eyes could not yet fully see, my nose confirmed.

The waning deep-forest light reflected off the leaves surrounding the mysterious patch, making it clear that this was the cynosure of the preserve. I felt my heart beating with excitement as I knelt beside a ramp to observe it closely. The stem was elongated and slim and gave way to drooping broad leaves. The elation we found in discovering this patch could only be surpassed by one thing—dinner, the next part of the adventure.

RAMPS
(ALLIUM TRICOCCUM)

When springtime comes around, every chef I know goes crazy for ramps. The moment you can smell fresh flowers and fresh-cut grass, the buzz begins. Foragers gather them to barter or sell to chefs who want to cook with them.

Ramps belong to the Allium family, along with onions, leeks, shallots, and garlic, and are native to the woodlands of North America. They have beautiful broad leaves and white or variegated red hued stems, with juicy white bulbs that are exquisite and tender. Their unique wild flavor complements acidic or rich fatty foods.

Due to high demand, ramp populations in certain areas are becoming scarce. They take seven years to grow from seed to fruition, so sustainable foraging is something I must stress. Of course, if you find miles of ramps, pick to your heart's content. But be aware that nature needs to replenish itself. The golden rule for foraging is only take what you need and leave the rest. Note on a map where you have harvested ramps, and look for other spots so that you can gather from several places rather than just one. If your property has moist soil and full to partial sun, you can look into transplanting a few plants to your own land and harvest them for years to come.

Appearance: Ramps have oval smooth-edged leaves, 4 to 12 inches long. There are usually two or three leaves per plant. Leaves are green, with either reddish purple or white stems and white bulbs.

Smell: Oniony and garlicky.

Taste: A mix of onion, leek, and garlic; pungent.

Habitat: Grow in clumps or clusters on the floor of mixed forests and under trees. Need full sunlight and moist, dense soil.

Region: Native to eastern North America and commonly found throughout the Appalachian Mountain region.

Growth Cycle: Perennial. New plants grow every seven years; all plants flower in late spring.

Prime Harvest Season: Late March to early June, depending on location.

Dangerous Lookalikes

Young skunk cabbage Funky, skunk-like scent. Leaves are large, broad, smooth, glossy, and heart-shaped and emerge as tightly rolled spirals. Stalk vary from light green to reddish purple.

Lily of the valley Leaves have no scent when torn. Slender, erect, purplish stem, bearing two or three lance-shaped leaves that are dark green with a smooth texture. Arranged in a basal rosette. Small, bell-shaped flowers present early in the season. Emerges after ramps. Often found growing in shady woodlands in the wild, but typically found around homes and old farm sites. No rootlets or bulb present when the plant is uprooted.

False hellebore No distinctive smell. Very ribbed leaves compared to ramps. Leaves grow to be broad in a whorled arrangement around the stem. Typically mistaken for ramps when the plant is young. Often found in floodplains, marshes, and swamps.

Dangerous lookalikes: False hellebore

Pesto is a versatile sauce with an excellent flavor, and it comes together quickly, making it one of my favorite go-to recipes. This version is unique, as it's made with foraged ramps, which give it a strong allium flavor that is balanced beautifully by the other greens. Traditional pesto relies on a bounty of summertime basil, but you can use any seasonal greens. Kale, for example, works great in the winter. If you have a nut allergy, pepitas (pumpkin seeds) work well as a stand-in for the pine nuts.

RAMP PESTO

1. Drain the ramps and squeeze them dry. Then coarsely chop into bite-size pieces. Set aside.

2. Bring a large pot of salted water to a boil. Add the pasta and cook according to the package directions until al dente, 9 to 10 minutes. Drain and transfer to a large bowl.

3. Meanwhile, transfer the ramps to a food processor; add the kale, pine nuts, nutritional yeast, garlic, salt, red pepper flakes, and lemon juice; and pulse until finely ground. (Alternatively, you can use a mortar and pestle.)

4. Add the olive oil, a few tablespoons at a time, to the processor and continue pulsing until incorporated. Pulse (or mash) until the pesto is vibrant and glossy.

5. Toss the pesto with the pasta and top with basil and grated Parmesan. Garnish with the sumac, edible flowers, and additional red pepper flakes and enjoy!

COOK'S NOTES

Blanching is a technique to preserve the flavor, color, and texture of food prior to cooking. To blanch a green, or mushroom, or nut, bring a medium or large pot of salted water to a boil. Fill a bowl with ice water. Place the food in the boiling water. Most greens require 2 minutes in the boiling water, or 3 minutes when extra fibrous, like collard greens. Mushrooms require 3 to 5 minutes, and nuts 2 to 3 minutes. If blanching a green, the leaves should be wilted but still vibrant in color. Immediately plunge the blanched food into the ice water for about 30 seconds to stop the cooking and then drain.

Toasting nuts intensifies their rich essence, creates a deeper color, and makes them crunchier. To toast nuts, preheat the oven to 350°F. Spread the nuts in an even layer across a baking sheet and place in the oven until they are golden and fragrant, 3 to 5 minutes, shaking once halfway through for even toasting. Alternatively, set a pan on the stovetop over medium heat, add the nuts, and toast until golden, 2 to 3 minutes, shaking the pan gently every so often to avoid burning.

MAKES 4 TO 6 SERVINGS

1½ ounces ramp leaves, blanched for 1 minute (see Cook's Note)

1 pound pappardelle or any dried pasta of your choice

¼ cup coarsely chopped kale, arugula, or fresh basil

3 tablespoons pine nuts, toasted (see Cook's Note)

2 tablespoons nutritional yeast or grated Parmesan, plus Parmesan for topping

2 garlic cloves, roughly chopped

½ teaspoon kosher salt

½ teaspoon red pepper flakes, plus more for garnishing

Juice of ½ lemon

½ cup olive oil

Fresh basil for topping

½ teaspoon dried sumac spice

Edible flowers (such as violets) for garnishing

RAMP KIMCHI

Kimchi is my preferred preservation technique for vegetables. It's a traditional fermentation method from Korea that makes vegetables taste incredible. Its spiciness comes from red pepper flakes, and the salty and slightly sour flavor, from the lacto-fermentation process. Kimchi is delicious on its own, but is also an excellent accompaniment to rice or fried eggs, or as a filling in a sandwich. I use Scotch bonnet chiles to incorporate my favorite Jamaican flavor, but you can substitute habaneros.

MAKES 4 CUPS

Special equipment: Vinyl gloves, a sterilized 1-quart mason jar (see page 15)

1 pound ramps, leaves and bulbs

½ medium head napa cabbage

¼ cup sea salt

About 1 cup filtered water

2 tablespoons Vegan Fish Sauce (page 79)

1½ teaspoons grated fresh ginger

2 tablespoons chopped Scotch bonnet chile, seeds removed

1 tablespoon red pepper flakes or gochugaru (Korean red pepper flakes)

1½ teaspoons pure cane sugar

4 ounces daikon radish, peeled and cut into matchsticks

4 medium shallots, trimmed and thinly sliced

2 green onions, white and green parts, finely chopped

1. Cut the ramps lengthwise through the bulb, and slice the bulbs into 1-inch strips. Transfer to a large bowl. Cut the cabbage lengthwise through the core into quarters. Cut the core out of each piece, and cut the leaves in half, lengthwise.

2. Add the cabbage to the ramps and sprinkle with the sea salt. Massage the salt into the ramps and cabbage until they soften slightly. Add enough tap water to cover the ramps and cabbage, then press down with something heavy, like a large can of tomato sauce. Allow to sit for 3 hours.

3. Rinse the ramps and cabbage well under cold running water, and allow them to drain in a colander for 30 minutes.

4. In a mortar and using a pestle, combine the filtered water, fish sauce, ginger, Scotch bonnet chile, red pepper flakes, and sugar and pound into a paste. Alternatively, combine in a food processor and process until smooth. Set aside.

5. Gently squeeze any remaining liquid from the ramps and cabbage and transfer to a medium bowl. Stir in the spice paste. Add the daikon, shallots, and green onions. Wearing gloves, mix the vegetables well until coated nicely with the spice paste.

6. Transfer the kimchi to a sterilized mason jar. Press down on the kimchi until liquid begins to rise and covers the vegetables. Make sure to leave at least 1 inch of headspace at the top of the jar and then seal it.

7. Put your jar of kimchi in a bowl or larger jar to catch any liquid that might leak out as it ferments, and allow it to sit somewhere cool and dark for 5 to 10 days. The longer the fermentation, the better. (After 2 days, you will see bubbles start to form in the jar, signaling that fermentation has begun.)

8. Open the jar to check the kimchi once a day and press the vegetables down with a clean spoon. The vegetables need to stay submerged in the brine so that the air bubbles from fermentation can be released. Feel free to taste and adjust the seasonings.

9. When the kimchi is fermented to your liking, seal tightly, and transfer to the refrigerator. If unopened, kimchi will keep for up to 1 year. Once opened, it will keep for up to 15 days.

Add this mouthwatering butter to your list of freezer staples! I like to smother vegetables with it, while my partner loves it on steak or chicken. No matter what you put it on, this recipe takes butter to the next level. It's savory, deep in flavor, and adds pizzazz to any recipe. If you aren't vegan, you may substitute dairy butter for the plant option. When you're ready to use the ramp butter, cut off what you need, bring to room temperature, and enjoy!

RAMP COMPOUND BUTTER

1. Squeeze the blanched ramps dry, then thinly slice, and transfer to a large bowl. Add the lemon zest and juice, herbes de Provence, salt, and cracked black pepper and stir to combine. Using a wooden spoon, work in the butter and mix well, until the ingredients are evenly dispersed in the butter.

2. Form the butter into four equal logs by rolling tightly in parchment paper. Unravel the parchment paper, then roll each log gently in the saffron (if using), edible flowers, and chives.

3. Re-wrap the logs tightly with parchment paper, twisting the ends, and place in a medium airtight container with a lid. Store in the refrigerator for up to 2 weeks. Or transfer to a large freezer bag and store in the freezer for up to 4 months.

MAKES 2 CUPS

3 ounces ramp leaves, ends trimmed, blanched for 30 seconds (see Cook's Note, page 27)

Grated zest and juice of 1 lemon

1½ tablespoons herbes de Provence

1 teaspoon flaky sea salt

1 teaspoon cracked black pepper

1 pound plant-based butter (such as Country Crock avocado oil) or dairy butter, cut into small chunks, at room temperature

2 teaspoons crumbled saffron threads (optional)

Edible flowers and fresh chives for garnishing

PORTOBELLO MUSHROOM STEAK WITH RAMP BUTTER

This simple weekday meal, with its umami flavor, is a palate pleaser. I love grilling year-round and enjoy grilling mushroom steaks, in particular, because they take on a smoky flavor and delicate char. If you don't have a grill, add a splash of liquid smoke to the recipe, and sear the mushrooms in a cast-iron skillet.

MAKES 4 SERVINGS

4 portobello mushrooms caps

½ cup olive oil, plus 2 tablespoons

¼ cup white wine

2 tablespoons balsamic vinegar

6 garlic cloves, minced

1 shallot, thinly sliced

1 teaspoon red pepper flakes

Kosher salt

1 pound creamer potatoes, halved

½ teaspoon cracked black pepper

½ teaspoon garlic powder

1 teaspoon onion powder

8 ounces green beans, trimmed

Juice of ½ lemon

Hot sauce for garnishing

¼ cup Ramp Compound Butter (page 31)

Flaky sea salt

Thyme and rosemary sprigs for garnishing

1. Preheat the oven to 450°F.

2. Gently wipe the portobello mushrooms with a wet paper towel to remove any grit or debris. Scrape out and discard the gills, and set aside the mushroom caps.

3. In a medium bowl, whisk together ¼ cup of the olive oil, the white wine, balsamic vinegar, garlic, shallot, ½ teaspoon of the red pepper flakes, and 1 teaspoon kosher salt.

4. Transfer the mixture to a large ziplock bag and add the mushroom caps. Seal the bag and shake vigorously to combine. Transfer to the refrigerator and let marinate for at least 30 minutes, or up to overnight.

5. Meanwhile, put the potatoes in a large bowl.

6. In a small bowl, combine ¼ cup olive oil, the remaining ½ teaspoon red pepper flakes, 1 teaspoon kosher salt, cracked black pepper, garlic powder, and onion powder and mix well. Add to the potatoes and toss to incorporate.

7. Transfer the potatoes to a heavy baking or roasting pan, cover with aluminum foil, and roast until fork-tender, about 45 minutes.

8. Meanwhile, in a large saucepan over medium heat, warm the remaining 2 tablespoons olive oil until it shimmers. Add the green beans, ½ teaspoon kosher salt, and the lemon juice. Mix, and allow the green beans to steam, mostly covered, until tender and juicy, about 5 minutes. Set aside.

9. Remove the marinated mushrooms from the refrigerator. Using tongs, place on the grill top or in a heavy-bottom skillet over medium-high heat. Sear the mushrooms for 3 minutes, flip, and sear the second side until fork-tender, 3 minutes more.

10. Thinly slice the mushrooms, or serve whole, gill side down, on each plate and add the green beans and potatoes. Top the potatoes with hot sauce to taste. Place 1 tablespoon of compound butter on top of each mushroom, and garnish with sea salt and a few sprigs of thyme and rosemary before serving.

FIELD GARLIC
(ALLIUM VINEALE)

Field garlic, commonly referred to as onion grass or wild garlic, is a delicious species of the onion family, and a common weed. It's native to many parts of the world, including Europe, Africa, and the Middle East, and has found its way to much of the eastern United States. This was one of the first wild plants that I learned to identify as a child, as it is easily distinguishable by smell. I often use it in place of chives (*Allium schoenoprasum*) when it is young and tender. If you are unsure about this plant, trust your nose! Every plant that smells like garlic or onion is edible.

Appearance: Looks like a clump of long grass from afar. It has long, tubular leaves (commonly known as "chives") and an underground bulb. The leaves are green, sometimes with a blue tinge.

Smell: Garlic forward.

Taste: Garlic forward, with a flavorful bulb.

Habitat: Grows in moist soil. Can be found in open fields, parks, lawns, meadows, woodlands, and moist sandy areas.

Region: Eastern North America as far north as Quebec, and west to Minnesota and Missouri.

Growth Cycle: Perennial.

Prime Harvest Season: Early April to July.

Dangerous Lookalikes: None.

Chutney is a condiment that's jam-packed with flavor from an array of herbs and spices. Chutneys are great because they provide a nice balance to a variety of dishes, and since they are preserved in vinegar and sugar, they last a long time. This one will go great with your favorite protein or vegetables!

WILD GARLIC CHUTNEY

1. In a food processor, combine the field garlic, cilantro, mint, shallots, rice vinegar, 2 tablespoons olive oil, lime juice, sugar, salt, and pepper and pulse until well blended but still chunky.

2. Transfer the mixture to a medium bowl and whisk in the remaining ½ cup olive oil.

3. Enjoy immediately, or store in a sterilized mason jar in the refrigerator for up to 2 weeks.

MAKES 1½ CUPS

Special equipment: Sterilized 12-ounce mason jar (see page 15)

1 cup tightly packed chopped field garlic, bulbs and chives

1 bunch cilantro

Leaves of 1 bunch mint

2 shallots, minced

2 tablespoons rice vinegar

2 tablespoons extra-virgin olive oil, plus ½ cup

Juice of 3 limes

2 tablespoons pure cane sugar

1 teaspoon kosher salt

1 teaspoon black pepper

"SCALLION" PANCAKES

Growing up vegetarian made dining out with friends challenging, as my options were limited. However, a local restaurant named China Dragon offered a delicious solution: scallion pancakes. Once I started cooking, this became one of my favorite, easy-to-make recipes. When foraging for field garlic, you often find large clusters, making it an easy, abundant harvest for pancakes.

MAKES 4 SERVINGS

Dipping Sauce

⅓ cup tamari or soy sauce

2 tablespoons rice vinegar

½ teaspoon hot sauce

1 tablespoon brown sugar

1½ teaspoons sliced field garlic chives

¾ cup cold water, plus more as needed

2 cups all-purpose flour, plus more for the work surface

1 teaspoon garlic powder

1 teaspoon kosher salt

¼ teaspoon black pepper

2 tablespoons sesame oil

20 field garlic chives, chopped

4 tablespoons vegetable oil

1. To make the dipping sauce: In a small bowl, combine the tamari, rice vinegar, hot sauce, brown sugar, and sliced garlic chives. Stir to blend well and set aside.

2. In a small pot over medium-high heat, bring ½ cup of the water to a boil.

3. In a food processor, combine the flour, garlic powder, salt, and black pepper. (Alternatively, whisk by hand and make a well in the center of the mixture.) With the food processor running, slowly add the boiling water to form a dough. (Or carefully pour the boiling water into the well in the bowl and gradually whisk into the dry ingredients.)

4. Slowly process (or stir) in the remaining ¼ cup cold water. The dough should feel slightly tacky to the touch. If it's dry, add additional water, 1 tablespoon at a time, until you can gather the dough into a smooth, round ball.

5. Transfer the dough to a lightly floured work surface and knead until it forms a cohesive ball, about 1 minute. Cover with a damp kitchen towel, and let rest for 30 minutes.

6. Cut the dough into four equal pieces. Remove one piece of dough, leaving the rest covered with the damp towel.

7. Roll out the dough into a thin rectangle, about 7 inches long and 4 inches wide. Brush with some of the sesame oil, and sprinkle one-fourth of the chopped chives evenly across the surface of the dough.

8. Roll the dough into a tight cylinder and then—this part is very important—coil it into a spiral, tucking the ends under the bottom of the coil.

9. Using the palm of your hand, flatten the dough; then, on a lightly floured work surface, roll it out into a 6-inch circle, about ¼ inch thick. Set this pancake aside, and repeat with the remaining three pieces of dough, sesame oil, and chives.

10. In a medium skillet over medium-high heat, warm 1 tablespoon of the vegetable oil until it shimmers. Add a pancake and cook, turning every 30 seconds to avoid burning, until golden and crispy around the edges, about 5 minutes. Repeat to cook the remaining pancakes. Cut the pancakes into wedges and serve, hot, with the dipping sauce.

Ackee is one of my favorite fruits and happens to be the national fruit of Jamaica. It has a red outer shell, yellow flesh, and large black seeds. Shockingly, its flavor is neutral rather than fruity, which you might expect, and its texture is very egglike. Ackee trees are evergreens, and grow abundantly in Jamaica, making their fruit a top foreagable in the country. In the States, you can usually buy it canned. Ackee and saltfish is one of Jamaica's most popular breakfast dishes, typically paired with ground provisions (a regional term for starchy root vegetables), fried dumplings, plantains, and a wild green called callaloo. Salt cod is traditionally mixed in with the ackee, but I use hearts of palm to make this vegan. If you can't find callaloo, typically sold canned in ethnic markets or in the international aisle of the grocery store, you can substitute spinach.

ACKEE & "SALTFISH" WITH FRIED PLANTAINS & CALLALOO

1. In a medium bowl, combine the hearts of palm and nori and add cold water to cover. Cover the bowl with plastic wrap and set aside in the refrigerator for at least 1 hour, or up to 8 hours.

2. In a large saucepan over medium heat, melt the butter and 2 tablespoons of the olive oil. Add the garlic, both bell peppers, onion, and tomato; turn the heat to medium-low; and cook, stirring occasionally, until the vegetables are tender, about 10 minutes.

3. Meanwhile, in a small saucepan over low heat, warm the remaining 2 tablespoons olive oil until it shimmers. Add the callaloo, ½ teaspoon salt, and ½ teaspoon pepper; cover; and cook, stirring occasionally, for 5 minutes.

4. Drain the hearts of palm and add to the bell pepper–onion mixture, along with the ackee, Scotch bonnet chile, thyme, cayenne pepper, and ¼ teaspoon black pepper. Mix well, cover, turn the heat to low, and allow to cook down for about 5 minutes.

5. Slice the plantains on a diagonal, ½ inch thick.

6. In a medium skillet over high heat, warm the neutral oil until it shimmers. Add the plantains in batches, so as not to crowd the pan, and cook until golden and crispy, 2 to 3 minutes per side. Drain on paper towels.

7. Serve the plantains alongside the ackee and callaloo.

MAKES 4 SERVINGS

One 14-ounce can hearts of palm, drained and shredded

One 4-inch nori sheet, crushed and then cut into tiny pieces or ground in a spice grinder, or 1½ teaspoons nori powder

3 tablespoons plant-based butter (such as Country Crock avocado oil) or dairy butter

4 tablespoons olive oil

6 field garlic bulbs, minced, plus 10 field garlic chives, chopped

1 medium red bell pepper, cored and diced

1 medium green bell pepper, cored and diced

1 small yellow onion, sliced

1 plum tomato, cored and diced

One 14-ounce can callaloo, or 8 ounces fresh spinach

Kosher salt and black pepper

Two 14-ounce cans ackee, drained and rinsed

1 Scotch bonnet chile, seeded and minced

Leaves from 3 thyme sprigs

¼ teaspoon cayenne pepper

2 overripe and blackened yellow plantains

2 tablespoons neutral oil (such as canola oil or avocado oil)

DANDELION
(TARAXACUM OFFICINALE)

Dandelions are incredible flowering plants because *every single part* is edible! They're easy to spot, making them yet another great wild edible to get started with on your foraging journey. Many people see dandelions as pesty weeds, but they're actually very beneficial. When dandelions show up on your lawn, they attempt to restore proper acidity and balance, loosen hard packed soil, and aerate the earth. The leafy greens are often cultivated and sold at supermarkets and farmers' markets for a hefty price, due to their health benefits. They help stimulate appetite, aid in digestion, and contain vitamins A, B, C, and D. So forage away! To gather dandelions, pick a few leaves, or use a knife to gently pry up the entire plant from soft soil.

Appearance: Bright yellow flowers, which grow up to 1½ inches in diameter. Have several rosette leaves, growing in a circular cluster, with irregularly toothed margins (edges). Leaf teeth face outward, away from the flower. A hollow stalk and milky sap, which releases from the stalk when the plant is mature.

Smell: Indistinct, neutral.

Taste: Slightly bitter and tangy.

Habitat: Prefer full sun but will also grow in partial sun. Can be found in lawns, open fields, meadows, and along path edges.

Region: Entirety of the United States and Canada.

Growth Cycle: Bloom twice a year, during spring and fall.

Prime Harvest Season: Early to late spring.

Dangerous Lookalikes: None.

Commonly known as "wish flowers," mature dandelions produce a spherical cluster of tiny feathery seeds that can travel for miles in the wind.

If you love a good, hot beverage, like I do, then you're in for a treat. Dandelion coffee isn't caffeinated like the real deal, but it has a unique taste that comes from the root of the plant. Not only are the flavors deep and reminiscent of regular coffee, but this drink has health benefits, as it's high in potassium and electrolytes. Enjoy plain, or with a splash of your favorite milk and sweetener!

DANDELION COFFEE

1. Preheat the oven to 350°F.

2. Clean the dandelion roots by scrubbing them with a brush under running water. Cut the roots into 1-inch pieces and spread out on a baking sheet.

3. Roast the roots until fragrant and dry to the touch, 30 to 45 minutes.

4. Transfer the dandelion roots to a medium pot and add the filtered water, lemon juice, cinnamon stick, and cardamom. Place over high heat, bring the mixture to a rolling boil, and cover. Turn the heat to medium-low and let simmer until very dark, like coffee, for about 15 minutes.

5. Strain the coffee through a mesh sieve, discarding all solids, and serve immediately.

MAKES 4 SERVINGS

1 cup dandelion roots

2 cups filtered water

Juice of ¼ lemon

One 3-inch cinnamon stick

2 cardamom pods

I've always viewed honey as nature's candy. Every batch has a unique flavor, which varies with the floral species of nectar that the honeybee collects. Dandelion honey serves as a vegan stand-in for those seeking the flavor and health benefits that come from consumption of honey produced by bees. Naturally produced honey is created by worker bees, which collect nectar and regurgitate it in their hives. To cure the nectar into honey, the moisture content must be reduced, so the honeybees flap their wings to control the humidity. Instead of the bees doing the work, you will, reaping the sticky-sweet reward. Use this as a one-to-one swap for standard honey in any recipe! First, you'll make the dandelion tea, which flavors the honey. Don't have the time to make the full recipe? Enjoy dandelion tea on its own—its flavor is super-floral and very pleasant!

DANDELION HONEY

1. To make the tea: In a small saucepan over medium-high heat, combine the dandelion petals, water, lemon slices, and vanilla bean. Bring the mixture to a medium boil, turn the heat to low, and let simmer for about 45 minutes. It should look yellow in color.

2. Remove the pan from the heat and let the tea steep at room temperature for at least 6 hours, or up to overnight. This allows the flavor of the dandelion flowers to infuse the tea, and thus, the honey.

3. After your dandelion tea has steeped, strain through a fine-mesh sieve or cheesecloth into a heavy saucepan; discard the solids.

4. Place the saucepan over medium heat and bring to a low boil. Add the sugar, gradually, stirring constantly and maintaining a low boil. Continue stirring until all the sugar has dissolved.

5. Turn the heat to low and let the honey simmer, uncovered, until it reaches the desired consistency, 45 minutes to 1 hour. Test the viscosity periodically; I like my honey slightly runny. Transfer the honey to sterilized mason jars.

6. Store the honey at room temperature or in the refrigerator for up to 2 months. Once opened, refrigerate to avoid any bacterial contamination.

MAKES 1 CUP

Special equipment: 2 sterilized 4-ounce mason jars (see page 15)

Dandelion Flower Tea

4 cups dandelion flower petals

2 cups water

3 lemon slices

½ vanilla bean, split in half lengthwise, or 1 teaspoon vanilla extract

2½ cups pure cane sugar

COOK'S NOTE

If you overcook the honey and it's too thick, add more water, 1 tablespoon at a time, over low heat until you can control the consistency again. Watch the mixture carefully, as it can quickly harden and turn into dandelion candy, due to the concentration of sugar and the evaporation of too much water.

DANDELION GREENS SALAD WITH STRAWBERRY BALSAMIC VINAIGRETTE

Dandelion greens can be bitter, but here the strawberries in the salad and in the dressing pair really well with the greens, making them good for you and incredibly tasty! This salad is a spring essential, as dandelions are abundant. White balsamic glaze has a tangy yet mild flavor with a cleaner aftertaste than traditional balsamic vinegar and is a pantry staple that I think everyone should have on hand, but a traditional balsamic reduction also works well.

MAKES 4 SERVINGS

2 cups strawberries, hulled and quartered

3 tablespoons white balsamic glaze

1 tablespoon olive oil

1 teaspoon kosher salt

½ teaspoon black pepper

1 teaspoon Italian seasoning

¼ teaspoon red pepper flakes

¼ teaspoon garlic powder

3 cups dandelion greens, rinsed and spun dry

2 tablespoons toasted white sesame seeds

½ small red onion, thinly sliced

1. Place ¼ cup of the strawberries in a small bowl and, using the back of a fork, mash them until smooth and juicy.

2. Add the balsamic glaze, olive oil, salt, black pepper, Italian seasoning, red pepper flakes, and garlic powder to the bowl and whisk well to combine. Set this dressing aside.

3. Coarsely chop the dandelion greens and transfer to a large serving bowl. Top the greens with the remaining 1¾ cups strawberries, sesame seeds, and red onion.

4. Pour the dressing over the salad and toss to combine before serving.

MAGNOLIA FLOWERS
(MAGNOLIA)

My mother and I share an appreciation for nature's endless beauty, and magnolia flowers are among the stunning spring blooms that bring us joy. These majestic flowers are large and aromatic, with white, pink, and purple blossoms, which have a gingery floral taste. They can be eaten fresh and raw, dried, or turned into a lovely simple syrup. In the United States, magnolias grow naturally only in the Southeast and in Texas. But they are a very popular ornamental tree, which makes them perfect candidates for urban foraging. I recommend getting permission before harvesting from a park or school grounds. Even if it's legal, people can be protective of the flowers, and you want to avoid any issues with security. Pluck one or two petals from each flower, so you don't detract from the beauty of the tree.

Appearance: Trees have glossy green leaves and stippled gray bark. Large floral star- or bowl-shaped blooms range from white to pink to purple.

Smell: Aromatic, sweet, slightly spicy.

Taste: Mildly gingery and floral; slightly rubbery in texture.

Habitat: Typically found in city parks, on school grounds, and along streets.

Region: Grow naturally in the southeastern United States from North Carolina to Florida and in Texas. Planted and cultivated throughout the country.

Growth Cycle: Perennial, with blooms returning each spring.

Prime Harvest Season: Early to late spring.

Dangerous Lookalikes: None.

The saucer magnolia (*Magnolia × soulangeana*) is known for its large, showy flowers that range in color from light to deep pink and sometimes even white. The blossoms are striking in appearance with large, cup-shaped petals when in full bloom.

Magnolia flowers have a gingery floral taste, which lends itself well to desserts. A simple syrup is a great way to preserve the essence of the flower, to remind you of spring's beauty year-round. And, as the name suggests, it's very simple to make!

MAGNOLIA FLOWER SIMPLE SYRUP

MAKES 1 CUP

Special equipment: Sterilized 8-ounce mason jar (see page 15)

2 cups magnolia flower petals
1 cup pure cane sugar
1 cup filtered water

1. Place magnolia flower petals in a small saucepan. Cover with the sugar and filtered water, place over medium-low heat, and bring to a simmer. Continue simmering, stirring constantly, until the sugar has fully dissolved, 3 to 4 minutes.

2. Remove from the heat and let the simple syrup cool for 30 minutes. Strain the syrup and discard the petals. Transfer to a sterilized mason jar.

3. The syrup can be stored, tightly sealed, at room temperature for up to 1 year. Once opened, it will keep for up to 2 months.

This cocktail is a spin on the Last Word, which is typically made with gin and Chartreuse, a liqueur that has been distilled by monks in France for centuries. Magnolia simple syrup brightens the original recipe with deep floral notes, which complement the herbal flavor profile of the Chartreuse and gin, making it the perfect drink! My partner loves making cocktails and introducing foraged elements into his creations. This was one of the drinks that we came up with after a foraging adventure. Cheers!

MAGNOLIA BLOSSOM COCKTAIL

1. Fill a cocktail shaker with ice and add the gin, Chartreuse, simple syrup, maraschino liqueur, and lemon juice. Shake until the shaker is very cold to the touch.

2. Strain the cocktail into two coupe glasses. Garnish each with a magnolia flower petal and lemon peel and enjoy!

MAKES 2 SERVINGS

Ice cubes for shaking

2 ounces gin

2 ounces Chartreuse

½ ounce **Magnolia Flower Simple Syrup (page 47)**

½ ounce Luxardo maraschino liqueur

Juice of ½ lemon, plus 2 strips lemon peel for garnishing

2 magnolia flower petals

MAGNOLIA BLOSSOM BUTTERCREAM CAKE

Outside of my foraging and regular chef adventures, one thing that I am known for are my cakes. People from all over my state have summoned me to make vegan cakes for various celebrations. And for good reason! It is quite difficult to create a dairy- and egg-free cake that holds together, remains moist, and is as delicious as a traditional cake. After trying many recipes, I've managed to create a cake that does just that.

MAKES 12 SERVINGS

Special equipment: Two 8-inch cake pans, stand mixer, and an icing spatula

¾ cup salted plant-based butter (such as Country Crock avocado oil) or dairy butter, at room temperature, plus more for the pans

1¼ cups plant-based milk (such as Oatly) or dairy milk

2 teaspoons lemon juice or apple cider vinegar

1¾ cups all-purpose flour

1 tablespoon flaxseed meal

2 teaspoons baking powder

1 teaspoon baking soda

½ teaspoon ground ginger

½ teaspoon ground cinnamon

1¼ cups pure cane sugar

1 cup unsweetened applesauce

1 tablespoon plus 1 teaspoon vanilla extract

Buttercream Frosting

1 cup plant-based butter or dairy butter, at room temperature

4 cups confectioners' sugar

¼ cup Magnolia Flower Simple Syrup (page 47)

Juice of 1 lemon

2 tablespoons plant-based milk or dairy milk

1 tablespoon vanilla powder (see Cook's Note) or vanilla extract

6 to 8 drops food coloring of your choice

1 cup magnolia flower petals

Candied lemon peel for garnishing

1. Preheat the oven to 350°F. Grease two 8-inch cake pans with butter or vegetable oil, line with parchment paper, and set aside.

2. In a liquid measuring cup, combine the milk and lemon juice. Allow to sit at room temperature until this vegan buttermilk is thick and curdled, up to 5 minutes.

3. Meanwhile, in a large bowl, combine the flour, flaxseed meal, baking powder, baking soda, ginger, and cinnamon and whisk to incorporate.

4. In the bowl of a stand mixer on medium speed, cream together ¾ cup butter and the sugar until light and fluffy, about 3 minutes. Beat in the applesauce and vanilla and mix until well combined.

5. Turn the mixer speed to low, add the flour mixture alternately with the buttermilk, one third at a time, and mix until well combined. Divide the batter between the prepared baking pans.

6. Bake the cakes until lightly golden, they pull away from the edges of the pans, and a toothpick inserted in the center comes out clean, 30 to 35 minutes. Let the cakes cool in the pans for 10 minutes. Remove from the pans, transfer to wire racks, and let cool completely. (If you have the time, freeze the cakes for 30 minutes to ensure they don't crumble while frosting.)

7. To make the frosting: Meanwhile, in a clean bowl of the stand mixer, combine the butter, confectioners' sugar, simple syrup, lemon juice, milk, vanilla, and food coloring. Beat on medium speed until the butter is no longer visible and all the ingredients are well combined.

8. Spread frosting on one cake layer, then top with the second layer. Spread frosting on the top and sides of the cake, smoothing as best you can.

9. Garnish the cake with the magnolia petals and candied lemon peel and enjoy!

COOK'S NOTE

Vanilla powder is made from dried ground and processed vanilla beans. It often has a more intense flavor than vanilla extract.

STINGING NETTLE
(URTICA DIOICA)

Nettles are common wild greens that grow in abundance and are known for their nutrient-dense properties. They provide one of the highest sources of protein from wild plants in North America. Additionally, they're rich in vitamin C, calcium, iron, and fatty acids and high in fiber. I love the taste, which is reminiscent of spinach but more complex. I've found fields full of nettle, and when I do, I blanch and freeze them to preserve the bounty. When collecting nettle, bring shears and be sure to wear thick gardening gloves and long sleeves, as the stingers can be an irritant to your skin. Harvest nettles before they get too large. Once they're taller than a foot, the leaves are no longer tender.

Appearance: Dark green leaves with toothed margins and pointy tips. Stinging hairs along the stalks and across the leaf surface.

Smell: Indistinct, neutral.

Taste: Spinach-like, punchy, bright, and peppery.

Habitat: Found in disturbed, nutrient-dense soil. They like moist habitats and thrive in full sun to partial shade. Often seen on road banks, riverbanks, and in open farmland and meadows. Do not do well in dry areas.

Region: Northeastern and central United States, the West Coast, and in Arizona, Nevada, Texas, and New Mexico.

Growth Cycle: Perennial.

Prime Harvest Season: Midspring, before flowering

Dangerous Lookalikes: None.

My friend Gerry, a fellow forager, has made a version of this wonderful tea for me quite a few times during the height of nettle season. It's delicious, refreshing, and not too sweet. Because this tea is cold-infused, it takes 12 hours to reach peak flavor, but it is every bit as herbal and delicious as you'd expect. For me, this is the perfect cold drink to bring on a hike. Sweeten it to your liking, and if you're looking to enjoy this in the summer, preserve the nettles by dehydrating them, so you can indulge all year long!

THAI BASIL & NETTLE ICED TEA

1. In a 2-quart mason jar, combine the stinging nettle, fennel, Thai basil, mint, tea bags, water, and maple syrup. Screw the lid on top and give it a good shake. Put in the refrigerator and let steep for at least 2 hours or up to 24 hours to properly cold-infuse.

2. Taste and adjust the sweetness to your preference. Remove the tea bags and strain the tea through a fine-mesh strainer, discarding the solids.

3. Store the tea in the refrigerator for up to 2 weeks.

COOK'S NOTE

To dehydrate nettles, spread the stems and leaves on a baking sheet and warm them slowly in a 175°F oven for 1 to 2 hours. Alternatively, if you have a dehydrator, set it to the lowest setting and dry the nettles for 12 to 18 hours.

MAKES 10 TO 12 SERVINGS

Special equipment: 2-quart mason jar

2 cups loosely packed stinging nettle, stems and leaves

½ fennel bulb, sliced

1 cup loosely packed fresh Thai basil leaves

¼ cup fresh mint leaves

2 Earl Grey tea bags

8 cups filtered water

¼ cup maple syrup, honey, or pure cane sugar, or as needed

NETTLE & JAMMY ONION GALETTE

I love a good galette, and this one is particularly stellar, with its combination of peppery nettle and sweet, jammy, slow-cooked onions. You get a nice combination of sweet and savory throughout. The pastry dough is perfect for any tart you may want to make—you wouldn't believe it's vegan—and the galette utilizes crispy shallots, which are my go-to addition to weeknight veggies and salads and often found in Asian markets.

MAKES 6 TO 8 SERVINGS

Pastry Dough

1¾ cups all-purpose flour, plus more for the work surface

¼ cup almond flour

1 tablespoon confectioners' sugar

½ teaspoon kosher salt

½ teaspoon black pepper

½ cup plus 2 tablespoons plant-based butter (such as Country Crock avocado oil) or dairy butter, cold, cut into cubes

⅓ cup ice water, or as needed

2 tablespoons vegetable oil

Filling

3 tablespoon extra-virgin olive oil

2 large Vidalia onions, thinly sliced

¼ teaspoon kosher salt

¼ cup balsamic vinegar

10 ounces stinging nettle, leaves and shoots, blanched for 5 minutes (see Cook's Note, page 27)

Grated zest of 1 lemon

3 tablespoons brown sugar

1 tablespoon melted refined coconut oil

¼ cup crispy shallots

Crumbled feta, fresh thyme, and red pepper flakes for garnishing

1. To make the pastry dough: In a food processor, combine the all-purpose flour, almond flour, confectioners' sugar, salt, and pepper and pulse for 10 seconds, just to evenly distribute the seasonings.

2. Add the butter to the food processor and process until a dough begins to form—at this stage, there should be sections that look like paste, and sections that appear as large crumbles. Scrape the bowl to redistribute the mixture and then pulse until the dough is crumbly, 10 to 15 seconds more. Transfer the dough to a large bowl.

3. In a small liquid measuring cup, combine the ice water and vegetable oil and then pour over the dough. Using a spatula or your hands, press the water into the dough, which should become slightly crumbly, yet cohesive. Using your fingers, grab a small piece of dough; if it stays together, it's ready. If it is still too crumbly, add a little cold water, 1 tablespoon at a time, until it's lightly tacky.

4. Form a tight disk with the dough, making sure not to overwork it, and cover with plastic wrap. Transfer to the refrigerator and let chill for at least 1 hour or up to 24 hours.

5. To make the filling: Meanwhile, in a large lidded skillet over medium-high heat, warm the olive oil until it shimmers. Add the onions and salt, cover, and cook, stirring occasionally, until golden and tender, about 20 minutes. Uncover; stir in the balsamic vinegar, nettle, and lemon zest; cook for 1 minute. Add the brown sugar and stir until melted, about 2 minutes. Remove from the heat and set aside.

6. Preheat the oven to 400°F. Line a baking sheet with parchment paper. Remove the pastry disk from the refrigerator and let it sit at room temperature for 5 minutes.

7. Transfer the disk to a floured work surface and, using a rolling pin, roll out the pastry until it is about ⅛ inch thick. Transfer to the prepared baking sheet. Using a fork, pierce the bottom of the dough all over.

8. Leaving a 2-inch perimeter around the edges, place the filling in the center of the dough and then fold the edges of the dough over the filling. Brush the coconut oil around the exposed dough.

9. Bake the galette until golden, 25 minutes. Remove from the oven and let cool for 15 minutes, then sprinkle the crispy shallots across the top and garnish with feta, thyme, and red pepper flakes. Serve the galette immediately.

STINGING NETTLE SOUP

This soup is warm, comforting, creamy, and, my oh my, delectable. If your diet is plant-based, like mine, use a heavy whipping cream alternative in this recipe. If you can't find it, use unsweetened, full-fat coconut cream instead, or make my favorite cashew crema (see page 116)! The soup will keep in an airtight container in the refrigerator for up to 3 days, or in the freezer for up to 6 months.

MAKES 8 TO 10 SERVINGS

Special equipment: Immersion blender or high-speed blender

4 tablespoons plant-based butter (such as Country Crock avocado oil) or dairy butter

2 tablespoons extra-virgin olive oil, plus more for garnishing

2 shallots, minced

Leaves of 3 thyme sprigs

2 bay leaves

1 teaspoon dried oregano

½ teaspoon garlic powder

¼ cup dry white wine (see Cook's Note)

4 cups vegetable broth

1¼ cups stinging nettle, leaves and shoots, roughly chopped

1 pound Yukon gold potatoes, peeled and quartered

2 celery stalks, minced

1 bunch green onions, white and green parts, chopped

Juice of 1 lemon

1 cup plant-based heavy whipping cream (such as Silk) or dairy heavy whipping cream, plus more for garnishing

1½ teaspoons kosher salt

¼ teaspoon black pepper

1. In a large stock or braising pot over medium heat, melt the butter and olive oil. Add the shallots, thyme, bay leaves, oregano, and garlic powder; stir; and cook until the shallots are pale gold and the herbs are aromatic, 2 to 3 minutes.

2. Add the wine to the pot and deglaze by using a wooden spoon to scrape up any browned bits on the bottom. Add the vegetable broth, nettle, potatoes, celery, and green onions. Give the soup a good stir, cover, and cook until the potatoes are fork-tender, 20 to 25 minutes.

3. Turn the heat to medium-low and add the lemon juice, whipping cream, salt, and pepper. Remove the bay leaves, then, using an immersion blender, blend the soup in the pot until smooth and creamy. (Or transfer to a countertop blender and blend until smooth.)

4. Serve the soup hot. Garnish each serving with a drizzle of olive oil or additional cream and enjoy!

COOK'S NOTE

For the wine, I recommend a dry varietal, such as Chardonnay or Sauvignon Blanc.

FIDDLEHEAD FERNS
(MATTEUCCIA STRUTHIPTRERIS)

I remember going to "fiddlehead island" with Dave, one of my foraging mentors. It's a magical place in Connecticut where ostrich ferns grow abundantly. There were small islands along the Housatonic River, reachable by canoe, which were filled with various species of fiddleheads—the tightly coiled fronds of young ferns, which have not yet unfurled and resemble the top of a violin. Being there reminded me why foraging can be so exhilarating. Ostrich fern fiddleheads are the only edible and tasty fern that grows in abundance. One of the most notable characteristics of this fern is a deep U-shaped groove in the stem. If you don't see this defining characteristic, you have not found an edible fiddlehead, so be sure to examine the stems closely.

To harvest, using a knife, cut one to three fiddleheads off each cluster, shaking off as much of the brown papery scales as possible, so cleaning will be easier. Be sure to fully cook fiddleheads before consuming, as they can cause gastrointestinal upset when improperly prepared. The taste is slightly sweet and pea-flavored, with grassy notes on the back end, and the texture is as crisp as a green bean. They are mild and very pleasant, like the freshness of spring, especially when eaten in combination with stinging nettle.

Appearance: Tightly coiled fern fronds. Slender stalks with a deep U-shaped groove running the length of the entire stalk on the inside of the stem. Completely smooth in texture, with no fuzz. Papery brown scales, loosely attached to the uncoiled ferns. Three to twelve fronds per cluster.

Smell: Fragrant, with aroma like black currants.

Taste: Pleasant and delicate, with notes of asparagus, peas, and green beans.

Habitat: Moist woodlands, river valleys, and roadside ditches.

Region: Native to eastern and central North America and Alaska. Also grow in Northern California.

Growth Cycle: Annual.

Prime Harvest Season: Early spring, April to May.

Dangerous Lookalikes: None in North America, although many fern species are bitter, hairy, and inedible.

Did you know? Fiddlehead ferns get their name from the unfurled fern's uncanny resemblance to a fiddle.

FIDDLEHEADS WITH ROASTED RED PEPPER SAUCE & TOASTY CHICKPEAS

In this dish, a smoky red pepper dressing and crispy roasted chickpeas complement the fiddleheads. It all comes together quickly and is healthful, packing a nice bit of protein in every bite. For me, the dressing, which has an acidic punch from balsamic vinegar, is what takes it over the top. I could eat this every day for lunch if I had an abundance of fiddleheads all year-round!

MAKES 2 TO 4 SERVINGS

Special equipment: High-speed blender

Crispy Roasted Chickpeas

One 14-ounce can organic chickpeas (see Cook's Note)

¼ cup olive oil

2 teaspoons garam masala seasoning blend

1 teaspoon smoked paprika

1 teaspoon red pepper flakes

½ teaspoon dried marjoram, oregano, or Italian seasoning blend

½ teaspoon kosher salt

¼ teaspoon black pepper

Roasted Red Pepper Dressing

One 10-ounce jar roasted red peppers

1 shallot, coarsely chopped

5 garlic cloves

¼ cup balsamic vinegar

1 teaspoon kosher salt

½ cup olive oil

2 tablespoons olive oil

2 cups fiddleheads, papery skins removed and fiddleheads blanched for 2 minutes (see Cook's Note, page 27)

1 small head red cabbage, cored and shredded

4 ounces stinging nettle, blanched for 5 minutes (see Cook's Note, page 27)

Kosher salt and black pepper

Minced fresh tarragon and parsley for garnishing

1. To make the roasted chickpeas: Preheat the oven to 425°F. Line a baking sheet with parchment paper.

2. Drain and rinse the chickpeas and pat dry with a paper towel. (This will ensure that the chickpeas are nice and crispy after roasting.) Transfer the chickpeas to the prepared baking sheet and toss with the olive oil, garam masala, smoked paprika, red pepper flakes, marjoram, salt, and black pepper.

3. Roast the chickpeas until golden and crispy, 20 to 30 minutes, gently shaking the pan to move around the chickpeas halfway through cooking. Set aside.

4. To make the dressing: Drain the red peppers, transfer to a high-speed blender, and add the shallot, garlic, balsamic vinegar, and salt. Blend on high speed until smooth and creamy. Transfer to a small bowl, and add the olive oil in a slow stream, whisking vigorously to combine.

5. In a large skillet over high heat, warm the 2 tablespoons olive oil until it shimmers. Add the fiddleheads, cabbage, and stinging nettle; turn the heat to medium; and sauté until lightly cooked, about 3 minutes. Remove from the heat, add the crispy chickpeas, and toss. Season with salt and black pepper. Drizzle the dressing over the vegetables and toss to combine.

6. Garnish with tarragon and parsley, and serve immediately.

COOK'S NOTES

You can substitute cannellini beans or butter beans for the chickpeas. And add or swap any veggies, as you see fit. For example, asparagus and broccoli work very well when added to this dish.

What they say about vegetarians and vegans being "carb-o-tarians" is kind of true. As a lifelong plant-based lady, pasta has always been a huge staple in my life. I could not imagine living without it! This dish is lemony and fresh, with an abundance of veggies, and since it comes together in fewer than 30 minutes, it's great for a light weeknight meal. A staple in my household every spring, it's a riff on one of the recipes that I used to make as a private chef and is a great dinner if you're trying to impress a date, or if you're having company over!

FARFALLE WITH WHITE WINE, GARLIC & LEMON ZEST

1. Bring a large pot of salted water to a rolling boil over high heat.

2. Meanwhile, in a large saucepan over medium-high heat, melt the butter. Add the garlic, lemon zest, red pepper flakes, and kosher salt, and turn the heat to medium-low. Cook, stirring often, until the garlic is fragrant and golden, about 3 minutes.

3. Add the fiddleheads, snap peas, and frozen peas to the pan, stirring to combine. Add the wine, turn the heat to medium-low, cover, and let simmer until the vegetables are tender, 10 to 15 minutes.

4. While the sauce simmers, add the pasta to the boiling water and cook until al dente, usually 8 to 10 minutes. Drain the pasta, reserving ½ cup of the cooking water. Add the pasta and cooking water to the sauce and toss to combine.

5. Serve the pasta immediately, garnishing each plate with flaky sea salt and red pepper flakes.

MAKES 6 TO 8 SERVINGS

½ cup plant-based butter (such as Country Crock avocado oil) or dairy butter

1 head garlic, minced

Grated zest of 3 lemons

1 teaspoon red pepper flakes, plus more for garnishing

1 teaspoon kosher salt

1 cup fiddleheads, papery skins removed and fiddleheads blanched for 2 minutes (see Cook's Note, page 27)

1 cup sugar snap peas, strings removed

½ cup frozen peas (do not thaw)

⅓ cup dry white wine

1 pound farfalle or fettuccine

Flaky sea salt

TEMPURA FIDDLEHEADS WITH SOY-SESAME GLAZE & CHILI CRISP

Delicate and crisp tempura fiddlehead ferns take center stage in this quick recipe. With their unique flavor and satisfying crunch, these seasonal greens are enhanced by a savory soy-sesame glaze, providing a burst of umami goodness. A touch of heat is added with the irresistible chili crisp, adding depth and a spicy kick to each bite. Prepare yourself for a quick and flavorful dish that celebrates the beauty of nature's bounty in every mouthwatering morsel.

MAKES 4 TO 6 SERVINGS

Special equipment: Deep-fry/candy thermometer

½ cup all-purpose flour, sifted

¼ cup chickpea flour, sifted

2 tablespoons cornstarch

1 teaspoon garlic powder

1 teaspoon onion powder

½ teaspoon paprika

¼ teaspoon cayenne pepper

½ teaspoon kosher salt

¾ cup ice water

4 cups vegetable oil

Soy-Sesame Glaze

¼ cup soy sauce

3 tablespoons miso

1 tablespoon rice vinegar

1 teaspoon sesame oil

One 1-inch piece ginger

2 tablespoons dark brown sugar or Dandelion Honey (page 43)

2 cups fiddleheads, papery skins removed

Chili crisp (such as Momofuku Chili Crunch) or chopped green onions (green parts only) for garnishing

1. In a medium bowl, combine the all-purpose flour, chickpea flour, cornstarch, garlic powder, onion powder, paprika, cayenne, and salt and whisk to incorporate. Add the ice water and whisk again until this batter is smooth and no lumps remain. Set aside.

2. In a medium heavy-bottom pot over medium-high heat, warm the vegetable oil until it reaches 350°F on the deep-fry/candy thermometer.

3. To make the glaze: Meanwhile, in a small saucepan over medium heat, combine the soy sauce, miso, rice vinegar, sesame oil, ginger, and brown sugar and bring to a boil. Cook, stirring occasionally, until thickened, about 5 minutes. Remove and discard the ginger and set the glaze aside.

4. In batches, dip the fiddleheads in the batter and fry them in the hot oil until golden and crispy, 3 to 4 minutes. Drain on paper towels and transfer to a platter.

5. Drizzle the glaze all over the fiddleheads or serve it as a dipping sauce on the side. Spoon a little chili crisp atop the fiddleheads as garnish and enjoy while hot!

GARLIC MUSTARD
(ALLIARIA PETIOLATA)

Garlic mustard is a great plant to forage, as it grows in abundance and is considered invasive across North America. It is a non-native, biennial herb originally from Europe. Garlic mustard boasts a very pleasant, garlic-like flavor. It's weather resistant, and sometimes grows during the winter in regions where the weather is more mild. All parts of the plant are edible and provide different flavors, making it quite an interesting wild edible. During its first year of growth, the leaves are closer to the ground and the stalks are small, while in the second year, the stalks grow tall and flower.

Appearance: Grows in a rosette. Kidney-shaped leaves, with scalloped margins and a netlike pattern of veins, look like violets. In spring, produces flower stalks with tiny white blossoms. Elongated seed pods, which form on the stalk, disperse throughout summer.

Smell: Faintly garlicky.

Taste: Garlic and mustard notes in the leaves, and horseradish flavor at the root. Becomes more bitter during the summer months.

Habitat: Garlic mustard prefers partial sun and light shade. It grows well in disturbed soils and can be found in city parks and fields.

Region: Across the Northeast, Midwest, and Northwest of the United States.

Growth Cycle: Biennial. Flowers in midspring.

Prime Harvest Season: Early spring through fall, when the flower stalks are tender.

Dangerous Lookalikes: None.

Garlic mustard is in the *brassicaceae* family, which explains why it looks similar to broccoli! The plant produces a "broccolette" type of shoot during its second year of growth.

One thing that many people don't know about garlic mustard is its root is an incredible horseradish duplicate. This recipe can be used instead of horseradish in dips, salads, and more. The flavor of the garlic mustard will be mild or strong, depending on how long you let the roots sit after chopping them. So taste test after 1 minute and again after 4 minutes to see how you prefer it. You can save the stems and leaves for another recipe or discard them.

GARLIC MUSTARD–ROOT "HORSERADISH"

1. Rinse and scrub the garlic mustard roots and trim any woody ends. Using the small holes on a box grater, grate the roots into a medium bowl. (Alternatively, chop them finely and transfer to the bowl.)

2. Let the roots sit until they have reached your desired depth of flavor, 1 to 4 minutes. Add the vinegar and salt and mix well. Transfer the mixture to an 8-ounce mason jar.

3. Store the "horseradish" in the refrigerator for up to 2 weeks.

MAKES 1 CUP

Special equipment: Sterilized 8-ounce mason jar (see page 15)

1 cup garlic mustard roots

2 teaspoons white wine vinegar or apple cider vinegar

1 teaspoon kosher salt

WHOLE-ROASTED CAULIFLOWER WITH GARLIC MUSTARD CHIMICHURRI

Everyone has their opinions on cauliflower. You love it, you hate it . . . or maybe you're like me and understand that a well-seasoned cauliflower is the key to fully enjoying this wonderfully versatile vegetable! This whole-roasted cauliflower dish is full of flavor due to the large slits made across the top and almost down to the base of the stalk, which allow the flavors to penetrate. The chimichurri takes the dish one step further. It's bold, bright, acidic, and garlicky. Trust me. I know the salt content looks like a lot and, please, adjust as you see fit. But in order to really spice this up from the outside in, it's important for the cauliflower to be well seasoned. Prepare for your taste buds to be excited! If you don't enjoy cauliflower, you can still make the chimichurri and enjoy it on your favorite protein.

MAKES 4 TO 6 SERVINGS

1 whole cauliflower, leaves removed

3 tablespoons tahini

3 tablespoons plant-based butter (such as Country Crock avocado oil) or dairy butter, melted

2 tablespoons extra-virgin olive oil

1 tablespoon harissa paste

1 teaspoon pure cane sugar

1 teaspoon smoked paprika

½ teaspoon chili powder

2 teaspoons kosher salt

½ teaspoon black pepper

1½ teaspoons chopped fresh mint

Chimichurri

1½ cups chopped garlic mustard leaves

¼ cup chopped fresh parsley

Grated zest and juice of 1 lemon

2 tablespoons red wine vinegar

4 garlic cloves, minced

½ teaspoon kosher salt

⅓ cup extra-virgin olive oil

Red pepper flakes, toasted pine nuts (see Cook's Note, page 27), and Parmesan cheese for garnishing

1. Preheat the oven to 375°F. Line a small, lidded, deep baking dish with aluminum foil and set aside.

2. Using the tip of a sharp knife, cut diagonal slits all over the top of the cauliflower head, stopping about 2 inches above the stem so it stays intact throughout cooking.

3. In a small bowl, combine the tahini, melted butter, olive oil, harissa paste, sugar, paprika, chili powder, salt, and pepper and whisk to incorporate into a marinade.

4. Carefully place the cauliflower in the prepared baking dish, florets-side up, and baste liberally all over the top with the marinade, working it through the slits. Pour any remaining marinade evenly across the top of the cauliflower and then sprinkle with the mint.

5. Cover the cauliflower tightly with foil, top with the lid, and place the baking dish in the oven.

6. Roast the cauliflower for 30 minutes, then remove the lid and foil. Turn the oven temperature to 400°F and roast until golden and crisp on the outside, 45 minutes to 1 hour.

7. To make the chimichurri: Meanwhile, in a food processor, combine the garlic mustard leaves, parsley, lemon zest and juice, red wine vinegar, minced garlic, and salt and pulse until mostly smooth, with some chunks. With the motor running, add the olive oil in a slow stream until well combined. (Alternatively, mash the ingredients in a mortar with a pestle and whisk in the olive oil.)

8. Drizzle the chimichurri over the hot cauliflower; garnish with red pepper flakes, pine nuts, and Parmesan; and serve immediately.

This recipe was inspired by a broccoli rabe dish that is a favorite with my friends and family. When I realized that blanched garlic mustard shoots have a flavor reminiscent of broccoli rabe, I tried to prepare it the same way, and was pleasantly surprised at how delicious the outcome was. During garlic mustard season, this recipe is my go-to side. The golden raisins complement the bitterness of the garlic mustard, champagne vinegar provides a nice acid profile, and Calabrian chiles add just the right amount of heat. The next time you're looking for a great veggie side, pick some garlic mustard to use in this recipe!

SAUTÉED GARLIC MUSTARD WITH GOLDEN RAISINS & CALABRIAN CHILE

1. In a large saucepan over medium heat, warm the olive oil until it shimmers. Add the garlic and red pepper flakes and cook until the garlic is fragrant and golden, about 2 minutes. Add the garlic mustard and sprinkle evenly with the sugar, salt, and black pepper. Using tongs, toss to combine.

2. Add the raisins, chile, and champagne vinegar to the pan and toss once more. Turn the heat to medium-low and cook until the garlic mustard is tender, 3 to 5 minutes. Transfer to a medium bowl and stir in the pine nuts.

3. Garnish the garlic mustard with Parmesan before serving.

MAKES 4 SERVINGS

¼ cup extra-virgin olive oil

6 garlic cloves, sliced

¼ teaspoon red pepper flakes

1 pound garlic mustard, stalks and leaves, blanched for 2 minutes (see Cook's Note, page 27)

1 teaspoon pure cane sugar

1 teaspoon kosher salt

¼ teaspoon black pepper

1 cup golden raisins

¼ cup finely chopped jarred Calabrian chile, or jalapeño chile

2 tablespoons champagne vinegar

1 cup pine nuts, toasted (see Cook's Note, page 27)

Grated Parmesan cheese for garnishing

JAPANESE KNOTWEED
(FALLOPIA JAPONICA)

Japanese knotweed is an invasive plant that grows abundantly, especially in the northeastern United States, where it is often found along highways and near park entrances. Young shoots possess characteristics that can be sweet, savory, or a little bitter on the back end. Foragers often use them as a one-to-one swap for rhubarb. There are optimal times for harvesting knotweed, when it will have the best taste and texture—crunchy, rather than stringy and fibrous. The plants grow alarmingly fast, so timing is everything. Knotweed is similar to bamboo in appearance. It is very difficult to eradicate, as the roots are very large and woody. The best way to harvest it is to use a sturdy pocketknife to cut across the plant an inch above where the shoot meets the ground.

Appearance: Green with red knobs at the joints of the shoot and red speckles on its skin. Bamboo-like shoots. The colors become more mottled and pale as the plant matures. At their prime, shoots less than a foot tall appear reddish purple, and the tips have tightly furled leaves. Tiny white droops of flowers (called panicles) appear in late summer. Older stalks have branching stems, which give way to heart-shaped leaves. They can grow from 4 to 8 feet tall.

Smell: Indistinct, neutral.

Taste: Sweet or savory, slightly bitter, with notes of rhubarb.

Habitat: Likes disturbed, rocky soils, and grows in both partial shade and full sun. Often found in community gardens and parks.

Region: Throughout most of the United States, up through Canada, except the arid Southwest, Deep South, and Rocky Mountains.

Growth Cycle: Perennial, with seeds that never germinate (it propagates through rhizomes).

Prime Harvest Season: Early to late spring.

Dangerous Lookalikes: Pokeweed, which has oval leaves and green berries that ripen to dark purple during the summer months. It often comes up a bit later in the season than knotweed, and has a smooth stalk, unlike knotweed, which has a notched stalk.

Dangerous lookalikes: Pokeweed

Brace yourself for some serious nostalgia! These strawberry knotweed tarts are a grown-up version of those fruit-flavored treats you popped in the toaster as a kid. This recipe lets knotweed shine in all its glory, as sweet strawberries and bitter knotweed come together to create a magical flavor. What I like best about this recipe is that once you get the tart dough just right, you can let your imagination run wild with ideas for different fillings. Reheat leftover tarts for a warm treat throughout the week. The leftover filling also goes great on toast!

STRAWBERRY KNOTWEED TOASTER TARTS

MAKES 8 TO 10 SERVINGS

Special equipment: 2 sterilized 8-ounce mason jars (see page 15)

Jam Filling

1½ cups strawberries, hulled and quartered

1 cup peeled Japanese knotweed, sliced in small chunks

2 cups pure cane sugar

1 tablespoon lemon juice

1 teaspoon vanilla extract

Tart Dough

1⅓ cups all-purpose flour, plus more for the work surface

½ cup confectioners' sugar

¼ cup cornstarch

½ teaspoon vanilla bean powder, or 1 teaspoon vanilla extract

½ teaspoon ground cinnamon

¼ teaspoon baking powder

⅛ teaspoon baking soda

⅛ teaspoon sea salt

¼ cup plant-based butter (such as Country Crock avocado oil) or dairy butter, cold and cut into small pieces, plus 2 tablespoons, melted

2 tablespoons vegetable oil

2 tablespoons plant-based heavy whipping cream (such as Silk) or dairy heavy whipping cream

¼ cup ice water

1. To make the filling: In a medium saucepan over medium heat, combine the strawberries, knotweed, cane sugar, lemon juice, and vanilla and stir to incorporate. When the filling starts to boil, turn the heat to medium-low, and cook, stirring occasionally, until thickened, 45 minutes to 1 hour.

2. Transfer the filling to the sterilized mason jars, screw the lids on tightly, and let cool to room temperature. The jam will keep in the refrigerator for up to 2 weeks, or in the freezer for up to 3 months.

3. To make the dough: Meanwhile, in a large bowl, combine the flour, confectioners' sugar, cornstarch, vanilla bean powder (if using), cinnamon, baking powder, baking soda, and sea salt and whisk thoroughly. Using your hands, work the cold butter into the dry ingredients until the dough is crumbly and moist. Slowly work in the vegetable oil, then the heavy cream (and vanilla extract, if using). On a lightly floured work surface, knead the dough for 3 minutes; it will start out slightly crumbly, so add the ice water, 1 tablespoon at a time, until it is no longer falling apart and forms a cohesive ball. Divide the dough in half, and form each half into a disk. Wrap each disk in plastic wrap, and refrigerate for at least 30 minutes, or up to 24 hours.

4. Preheat the oven to 350°F.

5. On a lightly floured work surface, roll out one of the dough disks into an 8-inch square, ¼ inch thick. Cut the square into three equal rectangles, and then cut each rectangle in half crosswise; a total of nine rectangles. Repeat with the other disk.

6. Brush nine pieces of dough with the melted butter. Spread 1 tablespoon of filling across each buttered rectangle, leaving a ¼-inch border. Place an unbuttered rectangle of dough on top of a jam-filled one. Using your fingers, seal the edges and then crimp with a fork. Using a pastry cutter or knife, trim any excess dough. Using the fork, pierce the top of each tart once in the center. Transfer the tarts to a baking sheet and let rest in the refrigerator for 15 minutes.

continued

Basting Glaze

1 tablespoon maple syrup

1 tablespoon plant-based milk
(such as Oatly) or dairy milk

Tart Icing

1½ cups confectioners' sugar

¼ cup plant-based heavy whipping
cream (such as Silk) or dairy heavy
whipping cream

1 tablespoon lemon juice

2 teaspoons vanilla extract

¾ teaspoon red food coloring

Crushed freeze-dried strawberries
or candy sprinkles for decorating

7. To make the glaze: Meanwhile, in a small bowl, stir together the maple syrup and milk. Set aside.

8. To make the icing: In a medium bowl, combine the confectioners' sugar, heavy cream, lemon juice, vanilla, and red food coloring and whisk until smooth and runny. Set aside.

9. Using a pastry brush, brush the glaze across the top of each tart. This will make the tarts appear shiny after baking.

10. Bake the tarts until golden, about 22 minutes. Transfer to a wire rack and let cool completely. Using a knife or a spoon, spread icing over each tart and decorate with freeze-dried strawberries or sprinkles.

11. Store the tarts, in an airtight container, at room temperature for up to 3 days, or in the refrigerator for up to 1 week.

Pickling is the easiest and best way to preserve foraged knotweed. Knotweed pickles are unique in flavor and delicious with everything! These pickles are light, refreshing, herbaceous, and earthy. This recipe is a quick pickling method; yours will be ready to eat in just 2 days.

KNOTWEED PICKLES

1. Cut the knotweed stems into 2-inch pieces and place in the mason jar.

2. In a medium saucepan, combine the water, vinegar, olive oil, sugar, salt, peppercorns, chiles, garlic, shallot, and fennel seeds. Set over medium heat and bring this brine to a gentle boil, stirring constantly, 5 to 8 minutes. Turn the heat to low and let simmer for 5 minutes more so the chiles thoroughly infuse the brine. Remove from the heat and allow to cool for 10 minutes.

3. Pour the brine over the knotweed in the jar. Seal and let cool to room temperature.

4. Transfer the pickles to the refrigerator and let sit for 2 days before indulging, to give the brine a chance to infuse the pickles. The pickles will keep in the refrigerator for up to 1 month.

MAKES ABOUT 3 CUPS

Special equipment: Sterilized 32-ounce mason jar (see page 15)

6 stems 10- to 12-inch Japanese knotweed

1½ cups filtered water

1 cup white wine vinegar or apple cider vinegar

1 tablespoon olive oil

2 tablespoons pure cane sugar

1 tablespoon kosher salt

1½ teaspoons black peppercorns

3 Scotch bonnet chiles

6 garlic cloves

1 shallot, minced

1 teaspoon fennel seeds

SUGAR KELP
(SACCHARINA LATISSIMA)

Sugar kelp is a yellowish brown marine algae that is widely cultivated in Asia and, increasingly, in the United States, where kelp farming has gained wide appeal because of its sustainability. This large, majestic seaweed grows in dense, aquatic forests and can be eaten raw or cooked. Kelp farming is helpful to ocean habitats due to the plant's ability to absorb nutrients and carbon dioxide, improving water quality and helping decrease ocean acidification. It's a highly sustainable practice, requiring no fertilizers, pesticides, or fresh water to thrive.

At the forefront of the movement in the United States is Atlantic Sea Farms, a Maine-based company that is owned and led by women. It employs local seafood farmers during the winter months, when they have little work or income, and has become the leader in US-grown kelp sales, which only account for 3 percent of total kelp sales in the United States, the rest being shipped in from overseas. Harvesting sugar kelp is interesting and fun, but wild kelp populations are beginning to decline, due to overfishing and rising water temperatures. So harvest sustainably and only take what you need.

Did you know that wild kelp can grow as long as 7 to 8 meters? In ideal conditions, kelp can grow up to 18 inches a day!

Appearance: Large seaweed with a broad blade, often described as leathery in texture, growing 16 feet, or even longer. Coloration is from yellowish brown to golden to olive-brown. Stipe (stem) is typically short and stout and very flexible. Frond is long and undivided, appearing frilly or undulated at the margin. The holdfast—the part of the plant that attaches to a host (ledge, dock, boulder, lobster trap lines)—is small compared to the rest of the plant, yet strong, with multiple branching fingers, and is the only inedible part.

Smell: Fishy, briny.

Taste: Mild, sweet or salty, umami flavor.

Habitat: Flourishes in cold to temperate waters in the ocean in sheltered locations, down to depths of 100 feet, and in shallower water, where it may be exposed at low tides.

Region: From Northern California to Alaska, along the North American Pacific coastline, and along the Atlantic coast from the Long Island Sound to the Gulf of Maine, where it is very common.

Growth Cycle: Perennial, with individual plants living from 2 to 5 years, and reproducing through spores.

Prime Harvest Season: Early to late spring.

Dangerous Lookalikes: None.

Fish sauce appears in many recipes. This vegan version utilizes fresh, local kelp for which the depth and umami flavor of fish sauce is known. This recipe will become a pantry staple. I promise, you'll use it often!

VEGAN FISH SAUCE

1. In a medium saucepan over medium-high heat, combine the kelp, all the mushrooms, tamari, mirin, brown sugar, miso, and salt and bring to a boil. Stir, turn the heat to medium-low, and let the sauce simmer for 1 hour. Remove from the heat and let cool to room temperature. Transfer the sauce to a blender and blend on medium speed until smooth and thick. Transfer to the mason jar.

2. Store the fish sauce, tightly sealed, in the refrigerator for up to 2 weeks. (Alternatively, you can freeze it in ice-cube trays, and store the cubes in a ziplock freezer bag or vacuum-sealed bag for up to 1 year.)

COOK'S NOTE

Swap an equal amount for conventional fish sauce in any recipe.

MAKES 1¼ CUPS

Special equipment: Sterilized 8-ounce mason jar (see page 15)

¾ cup finely chopped, loosely packed fresh sugar kelp

½ cup chopped shiitake mushrooms

¼ cup chopped oyster mushrooms

½ cup tamari or soy sauce

2 tablespoons mirin

1 tablespoon dark brown sugar

1 tablespoon white miso

2 teaspoons kosher salt

HEARTS OF PALM "CALAMARI" WITH SCOTCH BONNET MARINARA

This is the perfect calamari substitution—and you don't have to take my word for it! I have entertained many guests with this recipe and gotten comments such as "These taste so similar to the real thing!" Thank you, kelp, for providing the beautiful seaside flavors to this dish. For the hearts of palm, my go-to brands are Reese and Native Forest. They tend to stay intact and are a bit heartier than other brands I've tried. Scotch bonnet chiles are my favorite chile to cook with, and they are often used in Jamaican cuisine. This appetizer is entirely worth the extra effort and will impress your dinner party guests!

MAKES 8 SERVINGS

Special equipment: Spider strainer skimmer or slotted spoon, deep-fry/candy thermometer

5 inches fresh sugar kelp, finely chopped, or 1 ounce dried

1½ cups all-purpose flour

1 tablespoon Old Bay seasoning

1 teaspoon paprika

1½ teaspoons kosher salt

½ teaspoon black pepper

1 cup filtered water

Juice of 2 lemons

Two 14-ounce cans hearts of palm, cut crosswise into 1-inch pieces and cores removed

Scotch Bonnet Marinara Sauce

2 tablespoons extra-virgin olive oil

4 garlic cloves, minced

1 Scotch bonnet chile, pierced with a fork

2 dried bay leaves

1 teaspoon dried oregano

One 28-ounce can organic crushed tomatoes

1 medium yellow onion, halved

Vegetable oil for frying

Chopped fresh parsley for garnishing

Lemon wheels for garnishing

1. Line a baking sheet with parchment paper.

2. In a large bowl, combine the kelp, flour, Old Bay seasoning, paprika, salt, and black pepper and whisk to incorporate. Set aside.

3. In a medium bowl, stir together the filtered water and lemon juice. Place the hearts of palm in the lemon water and let soak for 10 minutes.

4. Using a spider strainer skimmer or slotted spoon, drain as much water as possible from the hearts of palm and transfer them to the flour mixture, tossing lightly to fully coat. Shake off any excess flour and place the hearts of palm on the prepared baking sheet. Refrigerate for at least 30 minutes, or up to 4 hours. Set aside the remaining flour mixture.

5. To make the marinara sauce: Meanwhile, in a large saucepan over medium-high heat, warm the olive oil until it shimmers. Add the garlic, chile, bay leaves, and oregano and cook until golden, about 2 minutes. Add the crushed tomatoes and onion, stir, and turn the heat to medium-low. Cook the sauce until reduced slightly, about 45 minutes, stirring every 5 to 10 minutes. Remove and discard the bay leaves and chile. Remove the sauce from the heat, cover to keep warm, and set aside.

6. Fill a heavy-bottom, deep sauté pan three-fourths of the way with vegetable oil, set over medium-high heat, and warm until the oil registers 330°F on a deep-fry/candy thermometer.

7. Remove the hearts of palm from the refrigerator, toss them once more in the reserved flour mixture, and return them to the baking sheet.

8. In batches, so as not to crowd the pan, fry the hearts of palm until golden, turning them with a spider skimmer, 2 to 3 minutes. Drain on paper towels and transfer to a plate. Garnish with parsley.

9. Serve the "calamari" hot, with the sauce and lemon wheels on the side.

CARROT LOX WITH BAGEL & CREAM CHEESE

I made this carrot lox for famed French chef Jacques Pépin's eighty-fifth birthday party, hoping it would impress the chef and the attendees. After trying my carrot lox and cream cheese bites, Jacques pulled me aside and introduced me to one of his peers, impressed by what I had created. He said, "Chrissy has taught me a lot about vegan cooking. The carrot lox is fantastic." I still remember the smile on his face and the delight that filled my entire body that night. This is a dish I urge you to try. It's flavorful, salty, smoky, and slightly sweet in all the best ways. Enjoy in place of traditional lox in any recipe!

MAKES 4 SERVINGS

Carrot Lox

1 cup fresh sugar kelp, minced, or two 4-inch nori sheets, crushed and then cut into tiny pieces or ground in a spice grinder

1 cup tamari or soy sauce

2 tablespoons neutral oil (such as canola oil or avocado oil)

2 tablespoons rice vinegar

1 tablespoon tomato paste

2 teaspoons liquid smoke

1 teaspoon smoked paprika

1 tablespoon smoked salt

½ teaspoon black pepper

10 large carrots, peeled into thin ribbons

Pickled Red Onion

1 red onion, thinly sliced

Juice of 2 lemons

1 teaspoon pure cane sugar

4 everything bagels, halved

8 ounces plant-based cream cheese (such as Tofutti or Violife) or dairy cream cheese

Chopped fresh dill, red pepper flakes, and capers (optional) for garnishing

1. To make the carrot lox: In a large bowl, combine the kelp, tamari, neutral oil, rice vinegar, tomato paste, liquid smoke, paprika, smoked salt, and black pepper and whisk to incorporate. Add the carrots, stirring to combine. Cover the bowl with plastic wrap, put in the refrigerator, and let marinate for at least 3 hours, or up to overnight. This will allow the carrots to absorb the flavors and become silky.

2. Preheat the oven to 375°F. Line a baking sheet with parchment paper.

3. Drain the carrots and transfer to the prepared baking sheet, reserving the marinade.

4. Bake the carrots, until fork-tender and wilted, about 10 minutes. Remove from the oven and let cool for 10 minutes. Then return the carrots to the bowl with the marinade. Put in the refrigerator for at least 1 hour before using, or up to 1 week.

5. To make the pickled red onion: Meanwhile, in a small bowl, combine the red onion, lemon juice, and sugar. Let sit at room temperature to quick pickle, 20 to 25 minutes, stirring occasionally as the onions become juicier. When the liquid has turned quite purple, they're ready. Cover with plastic wrap and transfer to the refrigerator for up to 3 days.

6. Toast the bagels and spread the bottoms with your desired amount of cream cheese. Layer at least four slices of the carrot lox on top of each one, followed by a few slivers of the pickled red onion. Garnish with dill, red pepper flakes, and capers (if using), and place the tops of the bagels on the dressed halves.

7. Serve the bagels immediately!

YELLOW MOREL MUSHROOMS
(MORCHELLA)

Morels are one of the most highly sought-after fungi. They are hollow and, with their honeycombed caps, look alien. They are also delicious. There are several species, but for the sake of easy identification, we'll focus on the more common yellow morel (*Morchella esculentoides*). Morels seem to blend into the forest floor, making them elusive. The good news is, where there is one morel, there are usually more. And they are one of the first and only mushrooms to pop up during the spring. When I began foraging, I'd ask people to share their morel spots with me—not because I had any intention of telling others—I was excited about this species and wanted to learn. Turns out, foragers really don't care to share their spots, for fear of overharvesting. But I will equip you with the knowledge to find your own morels!

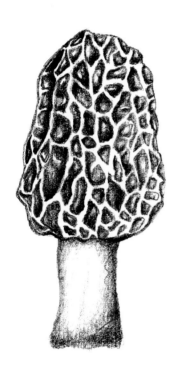

Appearance: Blond to yellow-brown with irregularly pitted, honeycomb-like surface. Cap attached to light- to medium-brown stem. Hollow when cut in half.

Cap: 4 to 5 cm wide and 7 to 9 cm high; oval to elongate. Pitted and appear spongelike. Blond to yellow-brown in coloration, sometimes appearing gray inside the pits. Attached to stalk at the base.

Stalk: 2.5 to 5 cm long, 1.5 to 2.5 cm thick. Often enlarged at base. Whitish with granular ribs. Hollow stalk appears white when cut open.

Spore Print: Spores are released from the pits of the morel, so cut in half lengthwise to obtain print. Morel spore prints are light in color, cream to pale yellow.

Smell: Earthy, natural.

Flavor Profile: Nutty, with a meaty texture.

Habitat: Typically grow on the ground close to elm and cottonwood trees. Often found in old fruit orchards and sometimes under tulip and ash trees. Often appear in areas previously disturbed by fire. Grow singly or in scattered groups, and sometimes in small clusters.

Region: Typically found in the Midwest, including Michigan, Ohio, Illinois, Indiana, and Missouri. In the eastern United States, through Pennsylvania, New York, and parts of New England. In the west throughout California, Oregon, and Washington. In Canada, they can be found in Alberta, Quebec, and Ontario and sporadically elsewhere.

Prime Harvest Season: July to August in the northeastern United States; June to September in the Southeast; September to November in the Northwest; November to February in California.

Dangerous Lookalikes: False morels, aka "toxic" morels, have a brain-like or wrinkled cap, typically appearing reddish brown to tan in color. Lack distinct pits or ridges of true morels. Cap loosely attached to stem and less hollow than true morels. White or creamy spore print.

MOREL "FRIED CHICKEN" BITES WITH DANDELION HOT HONEY

For this morel "fried chicken," with its crispy coating, perfection comes from the really great batter made with hot honey, to balance out the saltiness and pack the heat. This recipe capitalizes on the thin membrane of the morel mushroom, which crisps easily with the help of cornstarch. Morels should not be consumed raw, as they can cause an upset stomach. It's best to boil them before using in a recipe, or sauté them for a minimum of 10 minutes.

MAKES 4 SERVINGS

Special equipment: Deep-fry/candy thermometer, bamboo skimmer or tongs

Hot Honey

¼ cup Dandelion Honey (page 43) or plant-based honey (such as Un-honey) or bee honey

1 teaspoon red pepper flakes or cayenne pepper

½ teaspoon apple cider vinegar

Fried Morel Mushrooms

½ lemon

15 to 20 morel mushrooms, boiled in a pot filled with water for 10 minutes, and drained

1 cup all-purpose flour

¼ cup cornstarch

1 tablespoon Creole seasoning

1 teaspoon paprika

½ teaspoon dried oregano

Kosher salt

½ teaspoon black pepper

½ teaspoon cayenne pepper

Vegetable oil for frying

Chopped fresh thyme for garnishing

1. To make the hot honey: In a small saucepan over medium heat, combine the honey and red pepper flakes and stir to incorporate. Bring to a simmer, then remove from the heat. Stir in the vinegar and set aside.

2. To make the fried morel mushrooms: Line a baking sheet with parchment paper, line a plate with paper towels, and set both aside.

3. Squeeze the lemon half over the drained mushrooms. (This will add brightness and a nice acidic punch.)

4. In a shallow medium bowl, combine the flour, cornstarch, Creole seasoning, paprika, oregano, 1 teaspoon salt, black pepper, and cayenne and whisk to incorporate.

5. Dredge the morel mushrooms in the flour mixture, shaking off the excess, and place on the prepared baking sheet. Transfer to the refrigerator and let rest for 15 minutes. Then, if you wish, for a crispier bite, dredge the mushrooms in the flour mixture a second time.

6. In a medium heavy-bottom pot, warm 3 inches of vegetable oil until it registers 350°F on a deep-fry/candy thermometer. Add the mushrooms in batches and fry until they are golden brown, 2 to 3 minutes, making sure not to crowd the pan. (This will ensure that the oil does not cool quickly, and that the mushrooms are crispier and less oil logged.)

7. Using a bamboo skimmer or tongs, transfer the fried morels to the prepared plate to drain. When the last batch has drained, transfer to a serving plate. Garnish with thyme and sprinkle with additional salt.

8. Serve the mushrooms immediately with the hot honey.

One of my favorite ways to preserve morels is to pickle them. I make a quick brine that is acidic and slightly sweet. Morels are very soft and chewy, yet they become succulent and almost buttery when you pickle them. You can enjoy them as is, but they're also great on a sandwich.

PICKLED MORELS

1. In a medium pot over high heat, combine the water, vinegar, wine, garlic, shallot, peppercorns, mustard seeds, red pepper flakes, sugar, salt, and dill and bring to a boil. Add the morels, turn the heat to medium-low, and let simmer for 15 minutes.

2. Taste the morels and adjust the seasonings as needed, adding additional apple cider vinegar to increase a sour flavor profile, or more sugar for sweeter pickles. Divide among the sterilized mason jars, doing your best to evenly divide the solids as well as the liquid. Seal the jars and let cool to room temperature. Transfer the pickles to the refrigerator and let rest for 1 day before eating, to give the brine a chance to infuse the pickles.

3. Store the pickles in the refrigerator for up to 3 weeks.

MAKES 2 CUPS

Special equipment: 2 sterilized 8-ounce mason jars (see page 15)

2 cups filtered water

½ cup apple cider vinegar, or as needed

¼ cup white wine

4 garlic cloves

1 shallot, thinly sliced

10 black peppercorns

1 tablespoon mustard seeds

1 teaspoon red pepper flakes

1 teaspoon pure cane sugar, or as needed

1 teaspoon kosher salt

3 tablespoons chopped fresh dill

16 ounces morel mushrooms, blanched for 5 minutes (see Cook's Note, page 27)

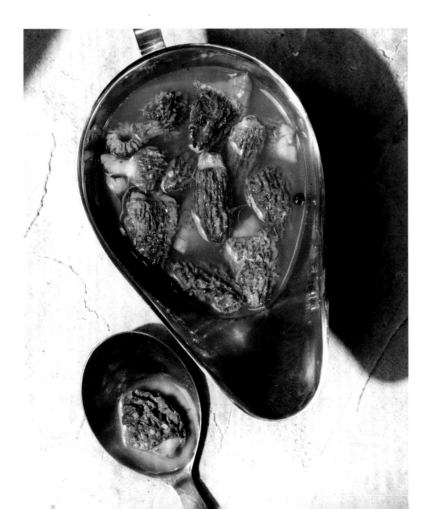

02

WELCOME, SUMMER

Summer signifies new life. "I'm here!" it shouts. Full of bright colors; warm sunshine, which kisses your skin; and the song of birds. Spring rains set in motion the growth of abundant fruiting fungi and lush green landscapes. For me, summer means endless woodland adventures with friends and foraging enthusiasts alike.

"Hop in the truck, let's get some snacks and head up to the Northeast Kingdom for the day. You're going to love it," said my friend Chris. I had just arrived in Burlington, Vermont, from Connecticut, in search of my favorite summer fungi: golden chanterelles. "Northeast Kingdom?" I replied. "That sounds magical."

The Northeast Kingdom is known for its pine forests, dirt roads, and the most beautiful landscapes you can imagine. It's where Vermont meets Canada. The drive there was spectacular, filled with laughter, great conversation, and beauty. We were surrounded by lush greenery, which was a welcome change from the drought conditions that I'd been experiencing at home. The day was warm, with the most refreshing breeze. We had the windows down the entire car ride and everything felt just right.

"We're almost there," Chris said with a grin. I could feel excitement pumping through my veins. We barely had any cell service, so he had to rely on Google map's terrain view to help us locate the forest of chanterelles. On the side of the road, I saw milkweed. A lot of it. "Do you mind if we stop so I can take a photo and harvest a few buds?" I asked in delight.

We pulled over, I got my photos, and deeply breathed in the fresh air in the peace and quiet of the nothingness that surrounded us. I peeped through the pine trees that lined the dirt road, giving way to gradients of the softest baby blues through the trees. I was overwhelmed with a feeling of belonging. We then set off to our destination—chanterelle heaven.

When we neared that spot, we took out our foraging knives and paper bags. Chris said, "Now, we are about to enter this forest. Be very careful where you step, alright? I want you to go ahead of me. Tell me what you see." I began cautiously. The forest was full of old pines, with a soft, dense moss floor. You could hear a pin drop; it was absolutely serene. I took another few steps before I saw a sight so breathtaking, I felt like I had won the jackpot: chanterelles as far as the eye could see. The gorgeous tiny mushrooms filled the forest floor with their light orange hue, so striking against the lush greenery. There must have been thousands.

The aroma of sappy pines filled my nostrils as we continued our trek. A porcini, one of the choicest edibles, peered out from the moss. It was pristine, and the first one I'd come across in person. Score! Our forage had just begun.

I'm always curious about people's stories. Chris had been on a sober journey for years. I didn't know his tale, and, honestly, felt it wasn't my business. But here in the peace of the forest, it felt right to talk about it. Timidly, I asked him, "How did you do it? You don't have to answer if you don't want. I'm just curious." With a big smile he replied, "Once I quit alcohol, the woods filled that void for me. I never looked back. Foraging provided the missing link that I was looking for. Being in the woods is all I need."

Embracing a new path and giving into the allure of curiosity saved my friend. Curiosity possesses the power to elevate a woodland day from pleasant to awe-inspiring, infusing your spirit with unexpected richness. I often say that nature serves as my dopamine fix. Every outing promises unpredictability; nothing is assured. You may go out on a quest to find a mushroom and leave the woods empty-handed. Yet, without fail, you will always leave with something—an experience to cherish forever.

Pictured here is a gorgeous beach dunes habitat in Cape Cod where you can often find beach plums and rose hips to forage.

CHANTERELLES
(CANTHARELLUS)

Many believe that, of all the fungi, chanterelles possess the highest culinary value across the board. There are numerous varieties of chanterelle mushrooms, but one of the most well-known and widely appreciated is *Cantharellus cibarius*, often referred to as the "golden chanterelle." Within the *Cantharellus* genus, there are several species that are recognized as chanterelles, each with its own unique characteristics and distribution. At this time, there are an estimated fifty to one hundred recognized species of chanterelles worldwide. This number continues to change as new species are discovered and scientific understanding evolves.

Chanterelles are wildly flavorful, making them a fun fungus to forage, especially since they tend to grow in abundance throughout the summer months. In this section, I cover golden chanterelles and black trumpets—two of my favorite types. Although both species are in the same family, there are slight differences. Black trumpets are often referred to as black chanterelles, but they are technically part of a different genus. One reason for this is because of the way the fruiting bodies physically connect to their hyphae (the branching filament structures that make up the mycelium of a fungus).

GOLDEN CHANTERELLE *(CANTHARELLUS CIBARIUS)*

Appearance: Smooth, trumpet-shaped caps. Rich golden color ranging from buttery yellow to warm apricot. The flesh pulls apart like string cheese. From 1 to 15 cm tall.

Cap: Smooth, slightly convex, becoming flat with in-rolled, wavy margin. From 1 to 15 cm wide. Apricot colored.

Stalk: From 2.5 to 7.5 cm long, 0.5 to 2.5 cm wide, and thick. Funnel-like in shape. Continuous with cap. Blunt ridges (also called "false gills") on underside descend to base of stalk. Ridges are thick, forked, cross-veined, and close together. Sometimes bruises deep orange. When cut open, flesh is solid and white. Smooth and paler in color at the base.

Spore Print: Spores are released from ridges. Spore prints are pale cream to pale yellow in color.

Smell: Notes of apricot.

Flavor Profile: Mild to spicy and peppery.

Habitat: Commonly found near hardwood trees such as beech, oak, poplar, and maple; or near conifers, such as pine or hemlock. Typically grow out of the ground in a symbiotic relationship with host tree species.

Region: Throughout North America.

Prime Harvest Season: July and August in the Northeast; June to September in the Southeast; September to November in the Northwest; November to February in California. Often plentiful after heavy rain during peak seasons.

Dangerous Lookalikes

Jack-o'-lantern mushrooms Toxic fungus that is bright orange to yellow-orange in color. True gills are close together on underside of caps, which are convex or flat with smooth texture. Found growing on decaying wood. Bioluminescent at night.

Scaly vase chanterelles Caps are covered with scales or flattened warts, appearing rough. Resemble a vase or inverted cone.

BLACK TRUMPET *(CRATERELLUS FALLAX)*

Appearance: Funnel-shaped caps with wavy edges. Velvety black or dark brown. Hollow, vase-like structure. From 3 to 14 cm tall.

Cap: Funnel-shaped, with wavy margins that roll outward. Smooth to slightly veined; varies in hue at different stages of growth, from brown to grayish. From 2 to 10 cm in diameter.

Underside: Smooth or slightly wrinkled. Scaly and dry. No gills, teeth, or pores present.

Stalk: Thin and delicate flesh. Trumpet- or horn-shaped and hollow, extending to the base of the foot. Slightly ribbed or grooved and waxy.

Spore Print: Spores are released from ridges. Ochre-buff to ochre-orange in color.

Smell: Fragrant, fruity, musky. You'll often smell these fungi before you see them.

Flavor Profile: Fruity, slightly reminiscent of black truffle.

Habitat: Commonly found on forest floors near hardwood trees, such as beech and oak, and near conifers, such as pine or hemlock.

Region: Throughout North America.

Prime Harvest Season: July through August on the East Coast; November through March on the West Coast; August through November in the Midwest.

Dangerous Lookalikes: None.

Dangerous lookalikes: Scaly vase

BLACK TRUMPET RISOTTO

Risotto is one of those dishes that fills me with a sense of culinary grandeur—though in reality, I'm crafting a beautifully simple rice creation. I've always adored a hearty mushroom risotto, and this rendition stands out with its unparalleled flavor. The elegant combination of black trumpets, white wine, and aromatic spices adds a special truffle-like touch to the dish. If you're feeling adventurous, you can toss in other fresh mushrooms too—shiitake and baby bellas are perfect choices. They bring a rich savory flavor that takes this risotto to the next level.

MAKES 4 TO 6 SERVINGS

2¾ cups vegetable stock

4 tablespoons plant-based butter (such as Country Crock avocado oil) or dairy butter

1 cup black trumpet mushrooms, roughly chopped

6 garlic cloves, minced

1 medium yellow onion, minced

1 shallot, minced

1 cup arborio rice

½ cup dry white wine

1 teaspoon kosher salt

¼ teaspoon black pepper

Chopped fresh oregano or chives and grated Parmesan for garnishing

1. In a small saucepan over high heat, bring the vegetable stock to a boil. Turn the heat to low to keep the stock hot.

2. In a medium pot over medium-high heat, melt 2 tablespoons of the butter. Add the mushrooms and sauté until slightly softened, about 2 minutes. Transfer to a small bowl and set aside.

3. In the same pot over medium-high heat, melt the remaining 2 tablespoons butter. Add the garlic, onion, and shallot; sauté until fragrant, about 30 seconds; and then add the rice. Turn the heat to medium and toast the rice, stirring constantly, until fragrant, 3 to 5 minutes.

4. Add the wine to the pot and deglaze, using a wooden spoon to scrape up any browned bits on the bottom. Let the wine cook off for about 3 minutes, stirring occasionally. Stir in the hot vegetable stock, ¼ cup at a time, making sure it's completely absorbed before adding more. Continue this process until all the stock has been absorbed, 25 to 30 minutes.

5. Fold the mushrooms into the rice, season with the salt and black pepper, and stir to combine.

6. Garnish the risotto with oregano and Parmesan, and serve immediately.

Delicata squash is mild, nutty, and sweet, making it an excellent base for "donuts." Trust me on this one. I know it sounds crazy, but these squash donuts are unlike anything you've ever experienced. The squash gets slow roasted in garam masala, cinnamon, and other warming spices, then doused in a black trumpet caramel. It's glorious. It's umami. It's sweet. It's rich with flavor in all the right ways. Make this once and you will certainly make it again.

DELICATA SQUASH DONUTS WITH **BLACK TRUMPET CARAMEL**

MAKES 4 TO 6 SERVINGS

1 delicata squash, ends trimmed, and seeded

¼ cup avocado oil

1 tablespoon garam masala spice

1½ teaspoons light brown sugar

1 teaspoon ground cinnamon

1 teaspoon kosher salt

½ teaspoon black pepper

½ teaspoon pink peppercorns, ground

Black Trumpet Caramel

1 cup pure cane sugar

6 black trumpet mushrooms, minced

¼ cup plant-based butter (such as Country Crock avocado oil) or dairy butter, at room temperature (see Cook's Note)

3 tablespoons unsweetened almond milk, at room temperature (see Cook's Note)

½ teaspoon kosher salt

1. Preheat the oven to 425°F. Line a baking sheet with parchment paper.

2. Cut the squash crosswise into ¾-inch-thick rings. Transfer to a medium bowl and toss with the avocado oil. Place the squash on the prepared baking sheet and set aside.

3. In a small bowl, combine the garam masala, brown sugar, cinnamon, salt, black pepper, and pink peppercorns and stir to incorporate. Sprinkle half the sugar-spice mix evenly across the squash rings, then flip them and sprinkle the second sides with the remaining seasoning.

4. Bake the squash until fork-tender, 20 to 25 minutes.

5. To make the caramel: Meanwhile, sprinkle the cane sugar in an even layer across the bottom of a small saucepan over medium heat. As the sugar begins to brown, shake the pan slightly to cook the caramel evenly, avoiding the sides of the pan as much as possible. Avoid stirring.

6. As the sugar becomes pourable and evenly caramelized, after about 5 minutes, using a heatproof silicone spatula, gently stir in the black trumpets and continue to cook until the color turns a deep caramel, about 3 minutes more. Whisk in the butter, and then slowly whisk in the almond milk, 1 tablespoon at a time, until it is fully combined. Remove from the heat and let rest for 5 minutes.

7. Transfer the squash to a platter, drizzle with the caramel, and enjoy!

COOK'S NOTE

The temperature of the butter and almond milk is important. If they are cold when added to the caramel, it may seize up, which you want to avoid.

GOLDEN CHANTERELLE TOASTS WITH ALMOND RICOTTA

This is an "any time of day" toast. My homemade almond ricotta has been one of my best-kept secrets, but I'm very happy to be sharing it with you. You can spread it on just about anything—it's great on savory crepes or in ravioli. Golden chanterelles shine in this recipe. Their sweet, nutty undertones complement the almond ricotta perfectly, and their chewy texture and silky consistency add a desirable touch to crispy, toasted bread. Fresh herbs brighten the flavor.

MAKES 4 TO 6 SERVINGS

Special equipment: High-speed blender

2 tablespoons plant-based butter (such as Country Crock avocado oil) or dairy butter

½ cup olive oil

5 garlic cloves, minced

1 teaspoon dried oregano

1 teaspoon onion powder

½ teaspoon paprika

¾ teaspoon black pepper

3 cups golden chanterelles

1 teaspoon kosher salt

3 tablespoons lager beer

Almond Ricotta

2 cups slivered almonds, blanched for 1 minute (see Cook's Note, page 27)

1 cup filtered water

2 tablespoons fresh lemon juice

1 tablespoon nutritional yeast

½ teaspoon onion powder

½ teaspoon garlic powder

½ teaspoon herbes de Provence

1 loaf ciabatta bread, cut into 12 to 14 equal slices

Fresh oregano and red pepper flakes for garnishing

1. In a large saucepan over medium-high heat, melt the butter with the olive oil. Stir in the garlic, oregano, onion powder, paprika, and ½ teaspoon of the black pepper and sauté until the garlic is golden brown, about 2 minutes.

2. Turn the heat to medium-low and stir in the mushrooms. Add the salt and remaining ¼ teaspoon black pepper, cover the pan, and cook, stirring occasionally, until the mushrooms are juicy and tender, 7 to 8 minutes.

3. Uncover the pan, turn the heat to medium, and add the lager. Allow it to cook off, about 2 minutes, then remove the pan from the heat and cover to keep the mushrooms warm.

4. To make the almond ricotta: In a blender, combine the almonds, water, lemon juice, nutritional yeast, onion powder, garlic powder, and herbes de Provence and blend on high speed until the mixture is smooth, thick, and creamy, scraping the sides down as needed, about 3 minutes. (If your blender is unable to handle processing the almond ricotta, add a little more water, 1 tablespoon at a time.)

5. Toast the bread, and smear some of the almond ricotta across each slice. Top with the cooked mushrooms, and garnish with oregano and red pepper flakes before serving.

This soup is luxurious and full-bodied in the best of ways. Chanterelles are cooked down in a flavorful broth with aromatics and spices, then deglazed with cognac. The cognac adds a deep caramel flavor that is sweet, fruity, and slightly bitter. It's easily what makes this dish so elegant. A lot of people say to use inexpensive liquor to cook, but I disagree. Use whatever is within your budget, of course, but try to find something that doesn't make you say "Yuck!" when you taste it on its own. Trust me on this one. It makes for better food, as a great-tasting liquor will add complex notes to any dish. (The Martell brand is very delicious in this recipe.) For this soup, when the cognac cooks off, you're left with the bare aromatics, which amp up the flavor of the delectable mushrooms. I like a little bit of added heat, so I sometimes drop a hot chile into the pot to simmer into the soup.

CHANTERELLE SOUP

1. In a medium stockpot over medium heat, melt the butter with the olive oil. Stir in the chanterelles, shallots, garlic, sage, thyme, cumin, and turmeric and sauté until fragrant and the vegetables are lightly browned, about 4 minutes. Stir in the brown sugar.

2. Add the cognac to the pot and deglaze, using a wooden spoon to scrape up any browned bits on the bottom. Continue cooking, without stirring, until the cognac is reduced by half. Pour in the vegetable stock, turn the heat to medium-high, and bring to a boil, stirring frequently. Turn the heat to low, cover the pot, and let simmer for 30 minutes. Uncover and add the flour and salt, whisking vigorously to combine. Stir in the cream, then remove from the heat and let cool for 5 minutes.

3. Using the immersion blender, blend the soup right in the pot until smooth, at least 30 seconds or up to 1 minute. (Or blend in a high-speed blender and return to the pot.)

4. Serve the soup hot, garnished with saffron and, if desired, red pepper flakes or edible flowers.

MAKES 4 TO 6 SERVINGS

Special equipment: Immersion blender or high-speed blender

2 tablespoons plant-based butter (such as Country Crock avocado oil) or dairy butter

¼ cup extra-virgin olive oil

2 cups golden chanterelles

2 shallots, minced

3 garlic cloves, minced

2 fresh sage leaves

Leaves of 2 thyme sprigs

½ teaspoon ground cumin

½ teaspoon turmeric

½ teaspoon brown sugar

½ cup cognac or bourbon

4 cups vegetable stock

2 tablespoons all-purpose flour

1½ teaspoons kosher salt

½ cup plant-based heavy whipping cream (such as Silk), dairy heavy whipping cream, or unsweetened coconut cream

Saffron threads, red pepper flakes, edible flowers (such as violets) for garnishing (optional)

PURSLANE
(PORTULACA OLERACEA)

Purslane is a juicy, creeping plant that reaches only a few inches in height. It spreads extremely fast, growing horizontally, and is thick and succulent. Purslane can propagate anywhere, from damp, rich soils to dry, sandy shores. It is renowned for its remarkable drought tolerance. It's one of the most undervalued and underutilized superfoods, rich in omega-3, which makes it especially valuable for vegans and vegetarians. Purslane is delicious and can be enjoyed raw. Make sure to harvest purslane only from clean, uncontaminated soil; use shears to snip the stem near the base of the plant.

Appearance: Thick, reddish, succulent stems and spade-shaped, fleshy green leaves, which grow 0.8 to 3 cm long. Grows horizontally, typically in 4- to 8-inch patches, and has yellow flowers, typically present through the entire harvest season.

Smell: Indistinct, neutral.

Taste: Slightly sour leaves. Fresh, juicy, crunchy, and bright.

Habitat: Damp soil, from farmlands to coastal shores. Also present in drier soils, and can be found on bluffs, along sidewalks, and in city parks. Prefers full sun and highly disturbed soils.

Region: Across the United States, with the exception of Alaska; southern Canada.

Growth Cycle: Perennial.

Prime Harvest Season: Late spring to early summer.

Dangerous Lookalikes: Spotted spurge. Unlike purslane, leaves are spotted, and when you snap the stem of a spurge plant, a milky substance will ooze out.

Dangerous lookalikes: Spotted spurge

PURSLANE SALAD

The best part of any salad is the crispy bits! This purslane salad includes freshly torn croutons, which I make with leftover bread. I love purslane because it offers a bright, springy crunch. And when paired with fresh tomatoes, crisp cucumbers, and a great dressing, you've got the ultimate salad. This is simple, delicious, and well balanced, and I could eat it on repeat. For the dressing, I re-created my mom's recipe, which is rich and flavorful and pairs perfectly with the salad.

MAKES 4 SERVINGS

Italian Dressing

½ cup olive oil

Juice of 1 lemon

1 teaspoon Italian seasoning

1 teaspoon onion powder

½ teaspoon garlic powder

½ teaspoon dried oregano

¼ teaspoon white pepper

1 teaspoon kosher salt

Torn Croutons

2 to 3 slices day-old bread, roughly torn into small chunks

2 tablespoons olive oil

½ teaspoon kosher salt

2 cups purslane, tender stems and leaves

1½ cups spinach

½ medium red onion, thinly sliced

1 cup cherry tomatoes

1 cup cucumber, thinly sliced

1. To make the dressing: In a medium bowl, combine the olive oil, lemon juice, Italian seasoning, onion powder, garlic powder, oregano, white pepper, and salt and whisk to incorporate. Set aside.

2. To make the croutons: Preheat the oven to 375°F. Line a baking sheet with parchment paper.

3. Spread the bread chunks on the prepared baking sheet and drizzle the olive oil evenly over the bread. Sprinkle with the salt and toss to combine.

4. Bake the croutons until golden and crispy, about 20 minutes. Stir once halfway through baking. Remove from the oven and let cool to room temperature.

5. In a large salad bowl, combine the purslane, spinach, red onion, cherry tomatoes, and cucumber. Drizzle all or most of the dressing over the salad, depending on your preference. Add as many croutons as you like, and toss to combine. Serve immediately.

Bruschetta is an Italian appetizer that is easy to make at home. This recipe uses all the ingredients of a classic version, but with a twist—the addition of purslane, which adds a bright, crisp element. For this recipe, I love using the Nonna Pia brand balsamic glaze, as it adds a nice sweetness to the bruschetta.

PURSLANE BRUSCHETTA

1. Preheat the oven to 400°F. Line a baking sheet with parchment paper.

2. In a large bowl, combine the purslane, tomatoes, 3 tablespoons of the basil, garlic, olive oil, and balsamic vinegar glaze and stir to incorporate. Season with salt.

3. Place the slices of bread on the prepared baking sheet, baste with the melted butter, and bake until golden and crispy, about 20 minutes, flipping them halfway through.

4. Top the toasted bread with the vegetable mixture, and garnish with the remaining 1 tablespoon basil. Serve immediately.

MAKES 8 TO 12 SERVINGS

1 cup purslane leaves

8 plum tomatoes, diced

4 tablespoons chopped fresh basil

3 garlic cloves, minced

2 tablespoons extra-virgin olive oil

1 tablespoon balsamic vinegar glaze

Kosher salt

1 loaf French or ciabatta bread, sliced ¼ inch thick

3 tablespoons plant-based butter (such as Country Crock avocado oil) or dairy butter, melted

LAMBSQUARTERS
(CHENOPODIUM ALBUM)

Common lambsquarters are a hearty, tasty wild green, similar to spinach and chard. It grows abundantly during the summer months across North America. Lambsquarters are often cultivated as an agricultural crop, yet are considered invasive. So snatch up as much as you can when you see them. One way to identify this plant is by the mealy white powder on young leaves. Their root systems are delicate, making them easy to uproot. When gathering, you can collect the whole plant. The seeds can be dried and milled into flour, and the leaves can be used in place of spinach. Lambsquarters can be eaten raw, steamed, boiled, or blanched. Like spinach, it shrinks down quite a bit during cooking, so be prepared to collect several cups!

Appearance: Pale grayish green leaves, coated with a powder, especially when young. First set of true leaves are opposite (paired). The rest join the stems in an alternating pattern. Upper leaves are smaller and elliptical; lower leaves are triangular with soft, rounded teeth. Stems are grooved and often tinged with purple. Grows in small, branching clusters. Small green flowers. Tiny black seeds when mature.

Smell: Indistinct, neutral.

Taste: Mild, spinach-like flavor.

Habitat: Disturbed soils such as fields, pastures, orchards, farmlands, vineyards, and roadsides. Thrives in empty lots and can sometimes be found in beach soil. Grows best in full sun and semimoist soil.

Region: Throughout North America.

Growth Cycle: Perennial, with seeds present from late summer into fall.

Prime Harvest Season: Midspring through early fall.

Dangerous Lookalikes: None.

I love the combination of rich, creamy layers of scalloped potatoes, topped with a crispy coating. Thinly sliced potatoes mean more flavor is absorbed by each slice. Serve this as an appetizer, and you'll be sure to impress your guests!

1. Preheat the oven to 350°F. Grease an 8-inch square baking dish with plant-based or dairy butter and set aside.

2. In a small saucepan over medium heat, combine the 3 tablespoons butter and flour, whisking often, until thickened into a roux, about 1 minute. Season with the thyme, salt, red pepper flakes, and paprika.

3. Turn the heat to medium-low, slowly whisk the milk into the pan and then stir in the lambsquarters. Stir the cheese into this sauce and cook until melted. Remove from the heat.

4. Place a layer of potatoes on the bottom of the prepared baking dish, and cover with a layer of sauce. Continue to alternate layers of potatoes and sauce, ending with a layer of sauce. Sprinkle the bread crumbs evenly over the top, and garnish with Parmesan and additional paprika.

5. Cover the dish with aluminum foil and bake until the potatoes are fork-tender, about 1 hour.

6. Serve the scalloped potatoes immediately.

SCALLOPED POTATOES WITH LAMBSQUARTERS & THYME

MAKES 8 TO 10 SERVINGS

Special equipment: 8-inch square baking dish

3 tablespoons plant-based butter (such as Country Crock avocado oil) or dairy butter, melted, plus more for the baking dish

2 tablespoons all-purpose flour

Leaves of 3 thyme sprigs, plus more for garnishing

1½ teaspoons kosher salt

1 teaspoon red pepper flakes

½ teaspoon paprika, plus more for garnishing

1¼ cups plant-based milk (such as Oatly) or dairy milk

1 cup lambsquarters leaves, coarsely chopped

¼ cup shredded, plant-based cheddar cheese (such as Violife) or dairy cheddar cheese

4 cups thinly sliced potatoes (use a mandoline if you have one)

½ cup bread crumbs

Grated Parmesan for garnishing

LAMBSQUARTERS CHICKPEA FLOUR FRITTATA

When I became vegan, I wasn't sure how to add protein to my diet, as I had relied on eggs and cheese as a vegetarian. Then I was introduced to chickpea flour, and my life became a lot easier. Chickpea flour is dense and full of protein. When combined with sautéed vegetables, it provides a mouthfeel similar to a traditional egg frittata. With a kick of spice, juicy cherry tomatoes, and lambsquarters, this frittata is a breakfast staple in my household. Add any vegetables you like. Broccoli and asparagus are excellent!

MAKES 6 TO 8 SERVINGS

¼ cup olive oil

10 cherry tomatoes, halved

½ red onion, thinly sliced

½ cup diced red bell pepper

½ cup diced green bell pepper

1 teaspoon onion powder

½ teaspoon garlic powder

1½ cups loosely packed lambsquarters

¼ cup minced Calabrian chile or jalapeño chile

2¼ cups plant-based milk (such as Oatly) or dairy milk

2 cups chickpea flour

1 teaspoon kosher salt

¼ teaspoon black salt (see Cook's Note)

½ teaspoon black pepper

Chopped fresh chives for garnishing

1. Preheat the oven to 375°F.

2. In a large cast-iron skillet over medium heat, warm the olive oil until it shimmers. Add the tomatoes, red onion, both bell peppers, onion powder, and garlic powder and sauté, stirring occasionally, until the bell peppers are softened, about 5 minutes. Turn the heat to medium-low, fold in the lambsquarters and chile, and sauté until wilted, about 4 minutes. Remove from the heat.

3. In a medium bowl, combine the milk, chickpea flour, kosher salt, black salt, and black pepper and whisk into a thick batter.

4. Add the batter to the skillet, stirring to combine with the sautéed vegetables. Cover the skillet with aluminum foil.

5. Bake the frittata until golden and crispy around the edges and soft at the center, 20 to 25 minutes. Garnish with the chives and serve immediately.

COOK'S NOTE

Black salt is a kiln-fired rock salt with a sulfurous, pungent smell reminiscent of eggs. It also tastes egg-like.

This dish is vibrant and wholesome—harmoniously bringing together tender braised lambsquarters, creamy butter beans, and aromatic dill. A brothy vegetable moment is always so satisfying to me, especially when it's light yet comforting, like this dish! With a tang from the rice vinegar, a hint of spice from red pepper flakes, and the richness of olive oil, this recipe is perfect for sharing with loved ones. Whether served as a satisfying main course or a flavorful side dish, it captures the essence of fresh and seasonal ingredients, celebrating the bounties of nature in a nourishing and delicious way. If you don't have butter beans on hand, any white bean will work well here.

BRAISED LAMBSQUARTERS & DILL WITH BROTHY WHITE BEANS

1. In a large skillet over medium heat, warm 2 tablespoons of the olive oil until it shimmers. Add the shallot and sauté until translucent, about 5 minutes. Add the garlic and red pepper flakes and cook until fragrant, about 1 minute more.

2. Add the lambsquarters to the skillet, stir well to coat, and cook until the greens begin to wilt, about 2 minutes.

3. Meanwhile, in a small bowl, combine the vegetable stock, rice vinegar, mustard seeds, and sugar and whisk until the sugar has dissolved.

4. Push the lambsquarters to the side of the skillet and add the remaining 1 tablespoon olive oil to the empty space. After a few seconds, pour in the vegetable stock mixture and stir to incorporate. Turn the heat to low, cover the skillet, and let the lambsquarters braise until tender, about 10 minutes.

5. Stir the butter beans and chopped dill into the lambsquarters and season with 1 teaspoon salt and ½ teaspoon black pepper. Re-cover the skillet and let cook so the flavors meld together, about 5 minutes more. Remove the lid and give the mixture a gentle stir. Taste and adjust the seasoning, if needed.

6. Serve the lambsquarters and butter beans hot, garnished with additional dill.

MAKES 4 SERVINGS

3 tablespoons olive oil

1 medium shallot, finely chopped

3 garlic cloves, minced

½ teaspoon red pepper flakes

4 cups packed lambsquarters, trimmed

½ cup vegetable stock

2 tablespoons rice vinegar

1 teaspoon mustard seeds

1 teaspoon pure cane sugar

One 15-ounce can butter beans, drained and rinsed

2 tablespoons fresh dill, chopped, plus more for garnishing

Kosher salt and cracked black pepper

OYSTER MUSHROOMS
(PLEUROTUS)

Oyster mushrooms are prized for their delicate flavor and known for their distinctive appearance. They are considered a choice edible and are perfect for vegan seafood dishes. Several types of oyster mushrooms are commonly cultivated and come in a wide range of colors including white, gray, yellow, and pink. A variety of oyster mushroom species pop up at different times of the year. I focus on two types—*Pleurotus pulmonarius*, a summer oyster, and *Pleurotus ostreatus*, which appears in the fall—giving you the opportunity to forage in multiple seasons! Oyster mushrooms are striking, and their shelflike growth makes them easy to spot in the woods. When harvesting, use a paper bag or a loosely woven bag with small holes, so that the mushrooms can continue dropping their spores and reproducing.

Appearance: Grow in overlapping clusters or shelves composed of smooth caps and gilled undersides attached to a short stalk. Fan-shaped to elongated ear-shaped. Summer oysters vary in color from white to cream to tan. Fall oysters range in color from cream to tan to grayish brown or olive.

Cap: Summer oysters grow less than 15 cm wide. Fall oysters grow up to 20 cm wide. Both species are fan shaped, with smooth, fairly meaty caps. Both have caps that grow in dense clusters.

Underside: Both species have gills that are closely spaced and run all the way down the stem. Slightly hairy by the base.

Stalk: Short, stout, solid, white, and hairy. About 0.5 to 1 cm long, and about 0.5 to 1 cm thick.

Spore Print: Oyster mushroom spores are released through the gills. Summer oyster mushrooms have a lilac-hued spore print. Fall oyster mushrooms have white spore prints.

Smell: Both smell pleasantly fishy and briny, and anise forward.

Flavor Profile: Both species are meaty and mild, yet fishy and delicate in flavor. Fall oysters tend to be firmer and meatier in texture compared to the more delicate summer species.

Habitat: Both species grow on living, dying, or dead trees, as well as stumps and logs. Oak, willow, and aspen trees are common hosts.

Region: Both types of oyster mushroom grow throughout North America.

Prime Harvest Season: Summer oysters pop up from late spring to early fall, sometimes fruiting twice. Fall oysters pop up from late fall to early winter, especially where the winters are mild.

Dangerous Lookalikes: Angel wings. To avoid mistaking oyster mushrooms for this unsafe doppelgänger, avoid rotting conifers, which angel wings favor. They are also stark white to ivory hued. Always take a spore print before considering consumption; an angel wing spore print is white. Symptoms of angel wing poisoning include tremors, weakness in the extremities, seizures, and mental turmoil and do not present until several days after consuming.

Oyster mushrooms are named for their resemblance to oysters in terms of shape and color.

OYSTER MUSHROOM TACOS WITH CILANTRO-LIME CASHEW CREMA

It's Taco Tuesday and you're looking for a new, exciting recipe. Oyster mushrooms are slow cooked in broth and seasonings, then topped with the most delicious Cilantro-Lime Cashew Crema. The mushrooms are so meaty in texture and become so flavorful that they will satisfy the deepest taco craving. In just under 30 minutes, you'll have an easy weeknight dinner! I've been guarding this cashew crema recipe, and am excited to finally share it with you. It's a staple I always have on hand.

MAKES 4 SERVINGS

2 tablespoons neutral oil (such as canola oil or avocado oil)

1 teaspoon ground cumin

1 teaspoon ground coriander

1 teaspoon chili powder

1 tablespoon tomato paste

2 cups oyster mushrooms, thinly sliced

1 tablespoon sofrito (such as Goya)

¼ cup vegetable stock

1 teaspoon browning sauce (see Cook's Note)

½ teaspoon kosher salt

Cilantro-Lime Cashew Crema

1 cup cashews, blanched for 3 minutes (see Cook's Note, page 27)

½ cup filtered water

Juice of 3 limes

1 bunch cilantro

½ teaspoon smoked paprika

1 teaspoon kosher salt

½ teaspoon black pepper

10 small tortillas (preferably corn), warmed

Thinly sliced red onion, sliced avocado, chopped fresh cilantro, and chopped tomatoes for garnishing

Lime wedges for serving

1. In a medium skillet over medium-high heat, warm the neutral oil until it shimmers. Add the cumin, coriander, and chili powder and toast for 30 seconds. Stir in tomato paste, and turn the heat to medium.

2. Add the oyster mushrooms and sofrito to the spice paste and stir to combine. Stir in the vegetable stock and browning sauce, add the salt, and turn the heat to low. Cover and let simmer until the mushrooms are fork-tender and have reduced in size by one-third, 8 to 10 minutes.

3. To make the crema: In a blender, combine the cashews, water, lime juice, cilantro, smoked paprika, salt, and pepper. Blend on high speed for 30 seconds, scrape down the sides of the blender, and blend again until smooth and creamy, 15 to 30 seconds more. (Transfer to an airtight container and store in the refrigerator for up to 4 days.)

4. Spoon the oyster mushrooms onto the tortillas, drizzle with the cashew crema, and garnish with red onion, avocado, cilantro, and tomatoes. Serve immediately with lime wedges for squeezing.

COOK'S NOTE

Browning sauce is a syrup-like savory sauce made from brown sugar. It enhances flavor and adds a rich deep color to food. It can be found in most supermarkets.

OYSTER MUSHROOM "FRIED CHICKEN" SANDWICH WITH COLLARD GREENS

Does this recipe take time? Yes. Is it worth it? Definitely! This is a riff on the first recipe that I ever developed on set for a *Bon Appétit* video, so you know it's a great one. Oyster mushroom clusters are doused in a buttermilk batter and fried to golden crispy perfection. Here, we are going to double dredge the mushrooms. My signature smoky collard greens are served on top with a special sauce.

MAKES 4 SERVINGS

Special equipment: Deep-fry/candy thermometer

Collard Greens

1 tablespoon plant-based butter (such as Country Crock avocado oil) or dairy butter

2 tablespoons olive oil

½ medium Vidalia onion, minced

3 garlic cloves, minced

1 teaspoon smoked paprika

½ teaspoon red pepper flakes

1 pound collard greens, chopped

1 teaspoon liquid smoke

3 cups vegetable stock

½ teaspoon kosher salt

¼ teaspoon black pepper

Spicy Sauce

¼ cup plant-based mayonnaise (such as Hellmann's vegan dressing) or regular mayonnaise

1 tablespoon hot sauce

1 teaspoon Dijon mustard

1. To make the collard greens: In a large pot over medium heat, melt the butter with the olive oil. Add the onion and sauté until softened, 3 to 5 minutes. Add the garlic, smoked paprika, and red pepper flakes, stirring to combine, and sauté until the garlic is fragrant.

2. Add the collard greens to the pot and stir to combine. Stir in the liquid smoke and then pour in the vegetable stock. Season with the salt and black pepper. Turn the heat to medium-low, cover the pot, and cook the greens until tender, 30 to 40 minutes. Set aside.

3. To make the spicy sauce: In a small bowl, combine the mayonnaise, hot sauce, and mustard and stir to incorporate. Set aside.

4. In a medium bowl, combine the milk and vinegar, whisk to incorporate, and let sit at room temperature for 5 minutes. This buttermilk will thicken and curdle slightly.

5. Meanwhile, in a separate medium bowl, combine the flour, Cajun seasoning, paprika, onion powder, garlic powder, cayenne, salt, and black pepper and whisk to incorporate. Set aside.

6. Using a damp clean kitchen towel, gently wipe the mushrooms clean to remove any dirt. Pat dry and trim the very bottom of each stem, making sure it remains attached to the cap, so the fried mushroom will be an intact "chicken." Cut the mushroom clusters into chunks, about three to four mushroom caps and stems per chunk. Soak the mushrooms in the buttermilk for 5 minutes.

7. Dredge the mushrooms in the flour mixture, dip in the buttermilk, and dredge again in the flour, and place on a clean plate.

8. In a medium heavy-bottom pot, over medium heat, warm 4 to 5 inches of neutral oil until it registers 350°F on a deep-fry/candy thermometer. Add the mushrooms, one or two at a time as to not overcrowd the pan, and fry until golden brown, 2 to 3 minutes. Using tongs, remove the mushrooms from the oil and gently shake to drain excess oil back into the pot, then transfer to a paper towel to drain.

9. Spread the spicy sauce on the bottom half of each roll, cover with a layer of fried mushrooms, and top with a layer of collard greens. Close the sandwiches and enjoy fresh and hot!

COOK'S NOTE

If you aren't vegan, you can replace the plant-based milk and cider vinegar with 1 cup dairy buttermilk.

1 cup unsweetened oat milk (such as Oatly) or almond milk (see Cook's Note)

1 tablespoon apple cider vinegar

1 cup all-purpose flour

1 teaspoon Cajun seasoning

1 teaspoon paprika

1 teaspoon onion powder

1 teaspoon garlic powder

½ teaspoon cayenne pepper

1 teaspoon kosher salt

¼ teaspoon black pepper

4 large clusters oyster mushroom (about 4 ounces each)

Neutral oil (such as canola oil or avocado oil) for frying

4 sandwich rolls (preferably brioche or potato buns), toasted

Oyster mushrooms have a fishy flavor, making them a marvelous alternative to seafood. In this recipe, artichokes are steamed and then filled with kelp- or nori-marinated oyster mushrooms. It's wonderfully pleasing on the palate, and the saucy red wine mignonette provides the perfect acidic complement. This dish is great for entertaining because it can be made ahead of time and served cold.

ARTICHOKE OYSTERS

1. Add enough water to a large pot to come just below a steamer basket. Season the water with half the lemon juice and 1½ teaspoons kosher salt. Set the steamer basket in the pot, set over high heat, and bring the water to a boil.

2. Remove and discard the tough outer leaves of the artichoke. Add the artichoke to the steamer basket, stem-side up; cover the pot and turn the heat to medium to keep the water at a steady simmer; and steam until fork-tender, 30 to 40 minutes. After steaming, pull the petals off the artichoke, discarding any discolored leaves, and set aside.

3. In a large, lidded skillet over medium heat, melt the butter with the olive oil. Add the onion and garlic and sauté until the onion is translucent and the garlic is golden, 2 to 3 minutes. Add the oyster mushrooms, kelp or nori, bread crumbs, and remaining lemon juice; season with ½ teaspoon kosher salt; and stir to combine. Cover the pan, turn the heat to medium-low, and cook for 5 minutes.

4. Add the vermouth to the pan and deglaze, using a wooden spoon to scrape up any browned bits on the bottom. Remove the mushroom mixture from the heat and let cool completely.

5. To make the mignonette: Meanwhile, in a shallow bowl filled with cold water, soak the red onion for 5 to 10 minutes and then drain. (This process mellows the flavor of the onion.) Transfer the onion to a small saucepan over medium heat and add the vinegar, sugar, red pepper flakes, and black pepper. Cook until the sugar has dissolved, about 5 minutes. Remove the mignonette from the heat and let cool to room temperature.

6. Place the artichoke petals on a large serving dish. Fill the bottom third of each petal with 1 tablespoon of the mushroom filling, garnish with parsley, and sprinkle with flaky salt. Spoon some of the mignonette atop each petal and serve with lemon wedges for squeezing.

COOK'S NOTE

This dish is also great cold. Just place all the components in the refrigerator for up to 24 hours to set. The flavors of the oyster mushrooms will deepen with time.

MAKES 10 TO 12 SERVINGS

Special equipment: Steamer basket

Juice of 2 lemons

Kosher salt

1 whole globe artichoke

6 tablespoons plant-based butter (such as Country Crock avocado oil) or dairy butter

1 tablespoon olive oil

½ medium yellow onion, minced

3 garlic cloves, minced

1½ cups oyster mushrooms, minced

1 tablespoon kelp or nori powder, or two 4-inch nori sheets, crushed and then cut into tiny pieces or ground in a spice grinder

¼ cup bread crumbs

¼ cup dry vermouth or white wine

Red Wine Mignonette

1 medium red onion, minced

¼ cup red wine vinegar

1 tablespoon pure cane sugar

½ teaspoon red pepper flakes

¼ teaspoon black pepper

Chopped fresh parsley for garnishing

Flaky sea salt

Lemon wedges for serving

CHICKEN OF THE WOODS
(LAETIPORUS)

Also referred to as "sulfur shelf," this choice edible is highly desired for its chicken-like flavor and texture. Enjoy these mushrooms smoked, in a stew, or as a chicken cutlet substitute. If you are new to foraging, chicken of the woods are also one of the easiest mushrooms to identify. They are considered a polypore fungus, meaning they have many pores, and they tend to be heartier—fleshy and tough—compared to other mushroom species. They are best harvested when young and tender, and since many of them grow on trees, a high-quality foraging knife with a curved blade is recommended. It will help you properly cut the mushroom away from the wood it is growing from. There are two types of chicken of the woods that grow in North America: *Laetiporus sulphureus*, which has sulfur-yellow pores and grows in a cluster of overlapping shelves; and *Laetiporus cincinnatus*, which has white pores, is more tender, and grows as a rosette. When collecting chicken of the woods, use a paper bag or a loose bag with small holes, so the mushrooms can drop their spores and continue reproduction.

Appearance: *Laetiporus sulphureus*, commonly known as sulphur shelf or chicken of the woods, displays shelf-like fruiting bodies with overlapping layers of vibrant yellow to orange caps. *Laetiporus cincinnatus*, also known as "white pored" chicken of the woods, looks like the sulfur shelf but with a more subdued pale white to creamy yellow cap. No true stalk.

Cap: From 5 to 30 cm wide. *Sulphureus* species commonly have overlapping, shelved clusters, which are flat and semicircular or fan shaped. Sulphur-yellow to pale salmon in coloration. *Cincinnatus* develops as a rosette of individual caps. Pale peach to salmon in coloration. Smooth.

Underside: Both species have a soft underside with small, sponge-like pores. *Sulphureus* species has sulfur-yellow pores, while *cincinnatus* species has white- to cream-colored pores.

Stalk: Chicken of the woods do not have a true stalk, but instead grow in shelf-like formations.

Spore Print: Spores are released through pores. White spore print.

Smell: Indistinct, mild.

Flavor Profile: Meaty, chicken-like texture; lemony notes; and subtly chicken-like flavor; sometimes slightly sour.

Habitat: Can be found on live, dead, or dying trees. Grows on stumps, tree trunks, and logs. Oak, cherry, and beech are common host trees, and occasionally, conifers. *L. cincinnatus* also grows on the ground.

Region: Florida north to eastern Canada, throughout the midwestern United States, the Pacific Northwest, and California.

Prime Harvest Season: Late spring through fall in most areas of the United States.

Dangerous Lookalikes: None.

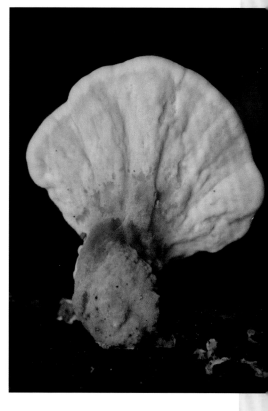

Young tender *Laetiporous sulphureus* growing on a decaying oak log.

CHICKEN OF THE WOODS BUFFALO DIP

My friend Shannon used to make a shredded Buffalo chicken dip. I tried it once when I was younger, and it was delicious. So I created a vegan version of the dip with the same textures, flavors, and mouthfeel that I remember. This dip works great with tortilla chips as an appetizer for a party or as a quick weekday snack!

MAKES 10 TO 12 SERVINGS

2 cups sliced chicken of the woods mushrooms

¼ cup plant-based butter (such as Country Crock avocado oil) or dairy butter

Juice of ½ lemon

1 bunch green onions, white and green parts, chopped

1 teaspoon pure cane sugar

1 teaspoon onion powder

½ teaspoon garlic powder

½ teaspoon kosher salt

½ teaspoon black pepper

One 8-ounce package plant-based cream cheese (such as Tofutti or Violife) or dairy cream cheese, at room temperature

½ cup ranch dressing

½ cup hot sauce

1 red bell pepper, thinly sliced

1 green bell pepper, thinly sliced

2 celery stalks, cut into 3-inch sticks

Tortilla chips for serving

1. Preheat the oven to 350°F.

2. In a large pot of salted water over high heat, boil the chicken of the woods until fork-tender, 8 to 10 minutes. Drain and set aside.

3. In a medium saucepan over medium heat, melt the butter. Add the mushrooms, lemon juice, green onions, sugar, onion powder, garlic powder, salt, and black pepper and sauté until fragrant, 2 to 3 minutes. Fold in the cream cheese, ranch dressing, and hot sauce. Turn the heat to medium-low and cook just until the cream cheese is melted and runny, about 1 minute.

4. Transfer the dip to a shallow baking dish and bake until the surface is slightly crackled and the texture is cohesive and semi-firm, about 20 minutes. Let cool for 5 minutes.

5. Serve the dip with the sliced bell peppers, celery, and tortilla chips.

The first time I made this dish, my partner, Levon, exclaimed, "Damn, this tastes like chicken!" And that, folks, is the power of tender, juicy, freshly harvested chicken of the woods. Katsu chicken is a Japanese-style crispy, shallow-fried chicken cutlet coated with panko (Japanese bread crumbs). This is my take on that dish, which I pair with a sweet-and-sour apple slaw and my version of tonkatsu sauce, which is a thick, flavorful brown sauce typically served with any katsu dish. If you want to save time and avoid making the tonkatsu sauce from scratch, you can use a thick teriyaki glaze instead.

KATSU CHICKEN OF THE WOODS WITH **APPLE SLAW**

1. In a large pot of salted water over high heat, boil the mushrooms until fork-tender, about 8 minutes. Drain and pat them dry, then set aside.

2. To make the apple slaw: In a small bowl, combine the cabbage, apple, rice vinegar, and lime juice and stir to incorporate. Set aside.

3. To make the tonkatsu sauce: In another small bowl, combine the ketchup, fish sauce, Worcestershire, and sugar and stir to incorporate. Set aside.

4. In a medium bowl, combine the chickpea flour, milk, rice vinegar, sugar, paprika, oregano, salt, black pepper, and white pepper and whisk to incorporate into a smooth, thick batter.

5. Spread the panko in a shallow bowl.

6. Dredge the mushrooms in the chickpea batter, and then in the panko, making sure they are well coated all over.

7. In a shallow medium sauté pan over medium-high heat, warm ½ inch of vegetable oil until it registers 350°F on a deep-fry/candy thermometer. Add the mushrooms, two at a time, and fry until golden and crispy, about 3 minutes per side. Using a skimmer, transfer to paper towels to drain.

8. Serve the fried cutlets immediately with the tonkatsu sauce and apple slaw.

MAKES 4 SERVINGS

Special equipment: Deep-fry/candy thermometer, bamboo skimmer or tongs

4 large, juicy chicken of the wood mushrooms

Apple Slaw

1 cup shredded red cabbage

½ cup julienned Honeycrisp or Granny Smith apple

¼ cup seasoned rice vinegar

Juice of ½ lime

Tonkatsu Sauce

3 tablespoons ketchup

2 teaspoons fish sauce (see page 79), or 1 teaspoon nori powder

2 teaspoons Worcestershire sauce (such as Annie's brand)

½ teaspoon pure cane sugar

1 cup chickpea flour

¾ cup plant-based milk (such as Oatly) or dairy milk

1 teaspoon seasoned rice vinegar

1 teaspoon pure cane sugar

1 teaspoon paprika

½ teaspoon dried oregano

1 teaspoon kosher salt

½ teaspoon black pepper

¼ teaspoon white pepper

½ cup panko

Vegetable oil for frying

CHICKPEA CURRY & GARLIC NAAN

Curry is a staple in Jamaican households, and I was introduced to it at a young age. My mom's curry was always my favorite. But to this day, I haven't been able to fully capture the essence of her flavor, even though I get my cooking style from her. She cooks with her heart and soul, not with a written recipe. If I ever ask her for one, I can be sure that all I'll receive are the main ingredients, without quantities or cooking times. I love that about her. This curried chickpea dish is an ode to my Jamaican heritage, and it gets close to my mom's in flavor. I like to serve roti with my curry, but it takes two days to make it properly. To save time, this naan does a great job of filling in. (I like to knead it on parchment paper for easy cleanup.) I hope you enjoy this taste of my Jamaican culture! You can find Jamaican-style curry powder at most grocery stores.

MAKES 6 TO 8 SERVINGS

Naan Dough

2 teaspoons instant yeast

1 cup warm water, or as needed

1 tablespoon maple syrup

2½ cups all-purpose flour, or as needed

1 teaspoon kosher salt

½ teaspoon garlic powder

Curry

¼ cup extra-virgin olive oil

½ medium Vidalia onion or another sweet onion, chopped

3 garlic cloves, minced

2 green onions, white and green parts, chopped

1½ tablespoons Jamaican hot curry powder (such as Blue Mountain)

One 28-ounce can chickpeas, drained and rinsed

1 cup diced chicken of the woods mushrooms

One 2-inch piece fresh ginger, peeled

1 Scotch bonnet chile, pierced with a fork

1 thyme sprig

continued

1. To make the naan dough: In a small bowl, combine the yeast, water, and maple syrup and stir to incorporate. Set aside for 5 minutes to allow the yeast to bloom. (It will have tiny bubbles and smell yeasty.)

2. In a medium bowl, combine the flour, salt, and garlic powder and whisk to incorporate. Make a well in the center and pour in the yeast mixture. Using a rubber spatula, stir the dry ingredients into the wet to form a soft, pliable dough. Using your hands, knead the dough into a smooth, round ball. If it feels a bit dry, add a little more tepid water, 1 tablespoon at a time, until the dough is slightly tacky, yet workable. Alternatively, if it is too tacky to work with, sprinkle lightly with additional flour. Cover the dough with a damp kitchen towel and place it in a warm location to rise until doubled in size, about 1 hour.

3. To make the curry: In a large heavy-bottom pot over medium-high heat, warm the olive oil until it shimmers. Add the onion, garlic, green onions, and curry powder and sauté until fragrant, 3 to 4 minutes. Add the chickpeas, chicken of the woods, ginger, fresh chile, thyme, vinegar, brown sugar, salt, black pepper, and MSG and stir to combine.

4. Add the vegetable stock to the pot, turn the heat to medium-low, cover, and cook for 8 minutes. Stir, turn the heat to medium-high, and stir in the sweet potato to submerge fully. Re-cover and cook until the sweet potato cubes are fork-tender, 15 to 20 minutes more. Add the coconut milk and stir to combine. Turn the heat to low and cook, uncovered, until the curry thickens up a bit, another 5 minutes. Remove from the heat and cover to keep warm.

CHICKPEA CURRY & GARLIC
NAAN CONTINUED

1 teaspoon white vinegar

2 teaspoons dark brown sugar

2 teaspoons kosher salt

½ teaspoon black pepper

1 teaspoon MSG

1½ cups vegetable stock

1 medium sweet potato, cubed

½ cup full-fat coconut milk
(including the fat at the
top of the can)

6 tablespoons plant-based butter
(such as Country Crock avocado
oil) or dairy butter

5. Meanwhile, on a lightly floured work surface, knead the naan dough by hand once more. Divide the dough into six equal pieces. Using a rolling pin, roll out each piece into an oblong shape about ⅛ inch thick.

6. In a medium skillet over medium-high heat, melt 1 tablespoon of butter. Add one naan and cook until bubbly and golden, 3 minutes per side. Transfer to a bread basket or a plate and cover with a kitchen towel to keep warm. Repeat with the remaining naan and butter.

7. Remove the Scotch bonnet chile and piece of ginger. Serve the curry immediately, with the naan alongside.

BEACH PLUMS
(PRUNUS MARITIMA)

I've spent a lot of time on Cape Cod chasing the most radiant and colorful sunsets, watching the way the moonlight twinkled on the ocean at night, and lying on a beach blanket with friends. Beach plum trees grow in abundance along the pristine white sand beaches of the Cape Cod National Seashore. If you take a walk there you may see many of these wild gems. They have gorgeous white blooms in springtime and early summer, before fruiting with juicy purple plums.

Appearance: Small bluish purple to crimson fruit, ranging in size from 1.2 to 2 cm in diameter, with a large pit.

Smell: Indistinct, however, when the shrub is in bloom, the flowers have a sweet scent.

Taste: Sweet and tart, with notes of strawberry, plum, and apricot.

Habitat: Grow on dense shrubs, 6 feet tall or more, with dark-green glossy leaves. Prefer semimoist soil, but also grow in gravelly and sandy soils, including sand dunes, typically near the coast. Prefer full sun.

Region: Seashores along the Atlantic coast, from Virginia north to Canada.

Growth Cycle: Perennial.

Prime Harvest Season: August to September.

Dangerous Lookalikes: None.

BEACH PLUM JAM

Beach plums are sometimes referred to as "preserve plums." Because of their small size and large pit, preserves are an easy way to enjoy the flavors of this sought-after fruit. All it requires is a few ingredients to make a tasty jam of your own.

MAKES 4 CUPS

Special equipment: 5 sterilized 8-ounce mason jars (see page 15)

5 cups ripe, soft beach plums, pitted

3 cups pure cane sugar

1 vanilla bean, split

Juice of 2 lemons

COOK'S NOTE

You can also transfer the finished jam to an airtight plastic container and store in the freezer for up to 1 year.

1. In a large heavy-bottom saucepan over medium-high heat, combine the plums, sugar, vanilla bean, and lemon juice and stir to blend. Bring the mixture to a boil, then remove the vanilla bean and turn the heat to medium low. Cover and let simmer for 30 minutes.

2. Uncover the pan and, using a potato masher or large spoon, mash the plums. Continue cooking the jam, covered, stirring occasionally, until thickened but still pourable, 30 to 45 minutes. Transfer to the sterilized mason jars, leaving 1 inch of headspace. Seal each jar with a lid and then let cool at room temperature.

3. The jam will keep in the refrigerator for up to 1 month.

I typically make a plum torte with store-bought plums, but this recipe became so much more interesting when I improvised with beach plums. Beach plums are more complex in flavor than cultivated ones, which is true of most forageable food. I consider this a tea cake, and it is perfectly acceptable to eat for breakfast, if you ask me!

BEACH PLUM TORTE

1. Preheat the oven to 350°F. Line an 8-inch springform pan with parchment paper.

2. Arrange the plum halves cut-side down across the bottom of the springform pan in a circular pattern, spacing them evenly.

3. In a medium bowl, combine both flours, the baking powder, cinnamon, nutmeg, and salt and whisk to incorporate.

4. In a stand mixer, or in another medium bowl and using a handheld electric mixer, on medium speed, cream the butter and cane sugar until soft, fluffy, and well combined, about 2 minutes. Add the dry ingredients and the applesauce in thirds, alternating between the two. Mix until the batter is smooth and almost pourable. Pour the batter over the plums.

5. Bake the cake until a toothpick inserted in the middle comes out clean and the cake is dense, golden, and slightly pulling from the edge of the pan, 55 to 65 minutes. Set the pan on a wire rack and let cool for 10 minutes, then release the spring, loosen the edges of the cake with a knife, invert onto the rack, remove the bottom and parchment paper, and let cool completely.

6. Dust the cake with confectioners' sugar before serving.

MAKES 8 TO 10 SERVINGS

Special equipment: 8-inch springform pan

20 to 30 ripe beach plums, halved and pitted

¾ cup all-purpose flour, sifted

¼ cup whole-wheat flour, sifted

1 teaspoon baking powder

½ teaspoon ground cinnamon

¼ teaspoon ground nutmeg

¼ teaspoon kosher salt

½ cup plant-based butter (such as Country Crock avocado oil) or dairy butter, at room temperature

¾ cup pure cane sugar

½ cup unsweetened applesauce

Confectioners' sugar for dusting

PORCINI
(BOLETUS EDULIS)

Porcini mushrooms are deeply umami in flavor, fluffy, and absolutely delicious! Also known as king bolete, they are one of the most sought-after mushrooms and are often sold at specialty and gourmet shops. They can be pricey, so why buy them when you can find them in the woods? Boletes can be quite difficult to identify and there are hundreds of species, but this particular variety is definitely worth learning about. It is often referred to as "penny bun" bolete due to its yeast-like smell and cap that resembles a bun. When gathering, cut the mushroom at the base, above the dirt, and place it in a paper bag or a bag with small holes so that the mushrooms can continue dropping their spores and reproducing.

Appearance: Large, varying brown-hued caps that are smooth, with thick, club-shaped or bulbous white stalks. Whitish to yellow pores beneath the cap.

Cap: From 8 to 25 cm wide. Can be from convex to flat in shape. Moist, sticky, and smooth. Reddish brown in color with a white line on the underside

Underside: White to yellowish pores beneath the cap are small and round.

Stalk: Typically 2.5 to 7.5 cm long, 4 to 10 cm thick, and white to brownish in color. Club shaped and thicker at the base of mushroom.

Spore Print: Spores are released from the pores. Spore prints are olive-brown.

Smell: Yeasty, bread-like.

Flavor Profile: Umami-rich, earthy, nutty, complex.

Habitat: Grow from the soil, typically in loose groups. Where you find one, there are typically others close by. Often found in conifer forests with spruce, hemlock, and pine trees, but can also be found in mixed woods.

Region: Throughout North America. Particularly abundant in the Pacific Northwest.

Prime Harvest Season: June to October.

Dangerous Lookalikes: False king bolete. A good way to tell the difference is that the pores of false king bolete stain greenish blue when cut, whereas king bolete pores do not.

Porcini is often referred to as "king bolete" among mushroom enthusiasts due to its impressive size, culinary value, and regal stature.

PORCINI MUSHROOM PÂTÉ

Pâté is a French delicacy—a mixture of seasoned ground meat and fat, typically duck liver or that of another animal. So how did I come to create this recipe? Well, I was on a mission to create the best vegetable banh mi (see page 141), which is a Vietnamese sandwich consisting of protein, pickled vegetables, spicy peppers, and, typically, a pâté. I wanted to get the pâté just right, so I improvised. Mushrooms are meaty enough to stand on their own, and they bring depth to the sandwich. This pâté is good as a spread, served on sandwiches, or used as a filling for a savory pastry. While most foraged mushrooms should be cooked, porcini are an exception to the rule and can be eaten raw.

MAKES 12 TO 14 SERVINGS

Special equipment: High-speed blender

1 cup fresh porcini mushrooms

½ cup walnuts or macadamia nuts, soaked overnight in water to cover (see Cook's Note)

2 garlic cloves

2 tablespoons lemon juice

2 tablespoons soy sauce

1 tablespoon neutral oil (such as canola oil or avocado oil) or butter

1 teaspoon nutritional yeast

½ teaspoon dried thyme

¼ teaspoon ground mace

1 teaspoon kosher salt

½ teaspoon black pepper

¼ teaspoon white pepper

1 to 2 tablespoons filtered water

1. In a blender, combine the mushrooms, walnuts, garlic, lemon juice, soy sauce, neutral oil, nutritional yeast, thyme, mace, salt, black pepper, and white pepper and blend on high speed. Add enough of the water to achieve a thick and almost smooth (with a few chunks) consistency, scraping the sides as necessary.

2. Store the pâté in an airtight container in the refrigerator for up to 1 week. Serve at room temperature.

COOK'S NOTE

Soaking the nuts overnight will ensure a smooth texture, which is essential to this recipe.

Banh mi traces its roots back to the fusion of French and Vietnamese culinary traditions during the colonial era, resulting in a harmonious marriage of crusty baguette and vibrant Southeast Asian flavors. I've taken the iconic Vietnamese delight and given it an irresistible twist that will leave you craving more. Picture succulent marinated jackfruit, soaking up all the vibrant spices and aromatics, nestled within a crusty baguette that's practically begging to be devoured. And don't forget the star of the show—crisp, tangy pickled veggies mingling with fragrant herbs, creating a symphony of textures and flavors.

BANH MI

1. To make the pickled vegetables: In a medium heatproof bowl, combine the daikon and carrot.

2. In a small saucepan over medium-high heat, combine the rice vinegar, water, sugar, and salt. Season with black pepper, bring to a boil, and cook until the sugar has fully dissolved, about 5 minutes. Pour this pickling liquid over the julienned vegetables. Transfer to the refrigerator and let soften, about 15 minutes.

3. Drain and rinse the jackfruit, discarding the seeds. On a cutting board, using a chef's knife, remove the coarse ends (or finely chop them) and then, using your hands, shred into a medium bowl. Pour the fish sauce over the jackfruit and stir until the jackfruit is fully immersed. Let marinate at room temperature for at least 15 minutes, or up to 24 hours in the refrigerator for more of a bold flavor.

4. In a medium sauté pan over medium heat, warm the neutral oil until it shimmers. Add the marinated jackfruit, Maggi Seasoning sauce, and brown sugar and cook until slightly thickened, 3 to 5 minutes. Remove from the heat and set aside.

5. In a small bowl, combine the mayonnaise and sambal oelek and hoisin sauce and stir to incorporate. Set aside.

6. Preheat the oven to 400°F.

7. Slice the baguettes in half lengthwise. Smother all cut sides with the mayonnaise mixture and place on a baking sheet. Toast in the oven until the edges are golden and crispy, about 3 minutes.

8. Spread the pâté lightly over half the bread. Layer each with half of the jackfruit, pickled veggies, cucumbers, green onion, jalapeño, and cilantro. Garnish with mint and cap with the remaining bread. Enjoy!

MAKES 2 SERVINGS

Pickled Vegetables

One 4-ounce daikon, peeled and julienned or thinly sliced

1 large carrot, peeled and julienned or thinly sliced

6 tablespoons rice vinegar

3 tablespoons filtered water

3 tablespoons pure cane sugar

1 teaspoon kosher salt

Black pepper

One 14-ounce can young green jackfruit in brine

¼ cup fish sauce (see page 79)

2 tablespoons neutral oil (such as canola oil or avocado oil) or olive oil

1 teaspoon Maggi Seasoning sauce

1 teaspoon brown sugar

½ cup vegan mayonnaise (such as Hellmann's vegan dressing) or regular mayonnaise

1 tablespoon sambal oelek

3 tablespoons hoisin sauce

2 small French baguettes, airy, rather than dense

1 recipe Porcini Mushroom Pâté (page 138)

1 small cucumber, thinly sliced

1 green onion, white and green parts, finely chopped

1 jalapeño chile, seeded

¼ cup fresh cilantro leaves

Fresh mint leaves for garnishing

LOBSTER FUNGI
(HYPOMYCES LACTIFLUORUM)

Commonly referred to as "lobster mushrooms," lobster fungi are not mushrooms at all. They are parasitic fungi that take over various mushrooms, commonly the *Russula* species, and form what we know as "lobster fungi." After it overtakes a species, the *Hypomyces* parasite forms a hard red shell. It is one of the best seafood replacements that I have found. Some are misshapen and white to yellow to light orange in hue, while others are bright orange to red and are quite majestic and easy to spot among leaf litter. They tend to be difficult to clean, so have a brush handy when you're ready to cook them. Harvest the fungi by cutting them at the base with a foraging knife, or by gently wiggling them out of the ground, making sure to brush off as much dirt and debris as you can in the field. If you come across lobster fungi that are soft and old, do not harvest them as they can make you ill. Always make sure to take a spore print! Although there have been no toxicity instances recorded, the fungi latch on to toxic hosts, including *Russula* species, and the possibility still remains.

Appearance: Hardy, firm, and dense. Pimpled orange-red surface, sometimes turning bright red with age. Irregularly textured, with no true gills. A hard red shell, with fine bumps across the surface. No true stalk.

Spore Print: White spores are released from pores. Spore prints are white as well.

Smell: Indistinct, mild.

Flavor Profile: Often fishy and seafood-like; range from bland to peppery, sometimes with hint of curry.

Habitat: Found in woods on *Russula* and white *Lactarius* mushroom species.

Region: Throughout North America.

Prime Harvest Season: Autumn in New England and the West Coast. Midsummer through early fall in the Midwest. Summer through late fall in the Pacific Northwest.

Dangerous Lookalikes: None.

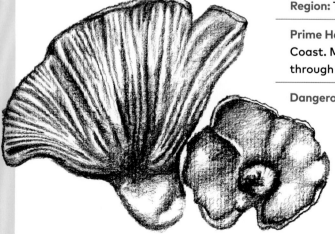

LOBSTER MUSHROOM ORECCHIETTE

In New England, lobster takes the summer season by storm. Every restaurant has some version of lobster pasta, and lobster rolls are abundant. I've never had lobster, but have been told that my take on it tastes quite similar to the real thing.

MAKES 4 TO 6 SERVINGS

1 pound orecchiette

½ cup plant-based butter (such as Country Crock avocado oil) or dairy butter

1½ cups coarsely chopped lobster mushrooms (½-inch pieces)

1 cup fresh corn kernels

2 green onions, white and green parts, sliced on a diagonal

6 garlic cloves, minced

1 tablespoon onion powder

1½ teaspoons nori powder, or one 4-inch nori sheet, crushed and then cut into tiny pieces or ground in a spice grinder

3 tablespoons plant-based heavy whipping cream (such as Silk) or dairy heavy whipping cream

1 teaspoon kosher salt

½ teaspoon black pepper

1. Bring a large pot of salted water to a boil over high heat. Add the orecchiette and cook until al dente according to the package directions, adjusting the cooking time to your preference. Drain and set aside.

2. In a large saucepan over medium-high heat, melt the butter. Add the lobster mushrooms, corn, green onions, garlic, onion powder, and nori powder and stir to combine. Turn the heat to medium-low and let simmer until the mushrooms are softened, 5 to 8 minutes.

3. Stir the cream, salt, and black pepper into the pan and mix well to combine. Let the sauce simmer for 1 to 2 minutes more, then remove from the heat.

4. Toss the pasta into the sauce, stir to combine, and serve hot.

These "lobster" rolls were a viral sensation on Instagram. They're *that* good. According to my food photographer, Natalie, they taste so similar to real lobster that you "wouldn't question it." Now, I'm not here to make everything taste like the real deal, but I find it interesting that we have the ability to imitate meat or fish using other foods from nature.

LOBSTER MUSHROOM ROLLS

MAKES 4 TO 6 SERVINGS

¼ cup plant-based butter (such as Country Crock avocado oil) or dairy butter

3 cups coarsely chopped lobster mushrooms (½-inch pieces)

1 tablespoon nori powder, or two 4-inch nori sheets, crushed and then cut into tiny pieces or ground in a spice grinder

1½ teaspoons Old Bay seasoning

¼ cup plant-based mayonnaise (such as Hellmann's vegan dressing) or regular mayonnaise

4 fresh chives, minced

1 tablespoon lemon juice, plus lemon wedges for squeezing

2 garlic cloves, minced

½ teaspoon kosher salt

¼ teaspoon black pepper

6 sandwich rolls, split

1 cup thinly sliced bib lettuce

Chopped fresh tarragon and paprika for sprinkling

1. In a medium saucepan over medium heat, melt the butter. Add the mushrooms and sprinkle with the nori and Old Bay seasoning. Stir and sauté for 5 minutes, then remove from the heat.

2. Pour off the remaining butter into a small bowl and set aside. Transfer the mushrooms to a medium bowl, put in the refrigerator, and let rest for 1 hour.

3. In a small bowl, combine the mayonnaise, chives, lemon juice, garlic, salt, and black pepper and stir to incorporate. Remove the mushrooms from the refrigerator, add the mayonnaise mixture, and toss to combine. Set aside at room temperature.

4. Preheat the oven to 350°F.

5. Brush the rolls with the reserved butter and place on a baking sheet. Toast in the oven until golden, about 5 minutes.

6. Layer the lettuce on the bottoms of the rolls and cover with the mushrooms. Sprinkle with tarragon and paprika and cover with the tops of the rolls.

7. Serve the lobster rolls with lemon wedges for squeezing.

JAPANESE WINEBERRIES
(RUBUS PHOENICOLASIUS)

Wineberries are the among the most beautiful, delicate, and abundant wild berries that I have ever had the pleasure of eating. They are not native to the United States; they were introduced from Asia. The berries of this bramble look like little gemstones, which stand out in the woods, and they taste like the raspberry's sweeter cousin. I look forward to wineberry season every year, as they star in some of my fondest early childhood memories of foraging. Lucky for me, I have a few bushes growing in my backyard. Wineberries are highly invasive, difficult to uproot, and pesky to harvest. Harvesting is a labor of love, as the season is short, the bushes are prickly, and it takes time to gather enough for a proper recipe. That said, I promise the reward is well worth it. I suggest gathering wineberries in a container rather than a bag, so that your berries stay intact until you get home (that is, if you don't eat them all before then!).

Appearance: Large, arching brambles growing as long as 8 feet; with hairy bristles, which are pinkish orange if plant is growing in full sun, and greener if growing in partial shade. Leaves are three-part and toothed, with a green upper surface and white undersides. Five-petaled white flowers are followed by bright, orange-red fruit, which changes color to a deep red once mature and ripe. Berries are in loose clusters.

Smell: Mostly indistinct, slightly fruity when berries are ripe.

Taste: Juicy, sweet, raspberry-like; notes of sherbet.

Habitat: Prefer moist habitats. Grow along edges of forests, fields, streams, and wetlands, and in open woods. Sometimes found along roadsides or in city parks. Prefer full or partial sunlight, but can be found in partial shade.

Region: From North Carolina north along the East Coast through eastern Canada. Also Tennessee and western Michigan.

Growth Cycle: Perennial, with seeds present from late summer into fall.

Prime Harvest Season: Midsummer.

Dangerous Lookalikes: None.

If I told you that collecting wineberries is a walk in the park, I'd be lying. I spend hours collecting wineberries every summer because they're *that* good. The problem with wineberries is that if you don't get to them quickly, when they're at peak ripeness, either the birds will eat them or they'll go bad. After all the work that goes into harvesting wineberries, you'll want to preserve them, and jam is the easiest way to do so. The grapefruit juice is a really lovely, tart addition to this jam, which enhances the flavor and adds a subtle, bitter edge.

WINEBERRY JAM

1. In a medium saucepan over medium-high heat, combine the wineberries, grapefruit juice, sugar, and cinnamon and bring to a boil. Continue boiling for 20 minutes, stirring occasionally. Using a potato masher or large spoon, gently mash the berries.

2. Check the jam for doneness by taking a small spoonful and placing it on a plate; the consistency should look slightly wrinkly and bounce back at the touch of a finger. If the jam is very runny, cook 5 minutes more and test again. Let cool to room temperature.

3. Transfer the jam to the sterilized mason jars, leaving 1 inch of headspace. Let cool completely and then seal each with a lid.

4. The jam will keep in the refrigerator for up to 3 months.

MAKES 4 CUPS

Special equipment: 4 sterilized 8-ounce mason jars (see page 15)

4 cups wineberries
Juice of 1 grapefruit
4 cups pure cane sugar
1 teaspoon ground cinnamon

COOK'S NOTE

You can also transfer the finished jam to an airtight plastic container and store in the freezer for up to 1 year.

Panna cotta literally means "cooked cream." It is a traditional Italian dessert that is usually made with gelatin, which, as a plant-based chef, is where my dessert woes lie. I tried panna cotta once when I was younger, before I knew it contained gelatin, and I really enjoyed its silky, creamy texture. For this recipe, instead of using gelatin, I use agar, which is a natural seaweed derivative that becomes gelatinous when heated. This dessert is so much fun to make, particularly because you can play around with how you plate it. I use silicone donut molds because I think they make the panna cotta look elegant and unique, but you can also use a muffin pan to set these tasty desserts!

PANNA COTTA WITH **WINEBERRY** COULIS

1. Grease the donut pan or muffin tin with dairy-free butter or butter.

2. To make the coulis: In a small saucepan over medium-high heat, combine the wineberries, sugar, water, and triple sec and bring to a simmer. Using a potato masher or large spoon, mash the berries. When the sugar has dissolved, turn the heat to low and cook until thickened, about 5 minutes.

3. Strain the coulis through a fine-mesh sieve into a small bowl, pushing the mixture through with a rubber spatula. Discard the seeds and solids and set the coulis aside.

4. To make the panna cotta: In a medium saucepan over medium-high heat, combine the coconut cream, white chocolate, milk, sugar, agar powder, and vanilla and whisk until well combined. Bring the mixture to a boil, then turn the heat to low and let simmer for 5 minutes. Turn the heat to medium-high and return to a boil to activate the agar. The mixture should become quite thick, yet pourable. (Watch it carefully; the panna cotta is ready when you insert a spoon into the mixture, pull it out, and the panna cotta solidifies within 15 seconds.) Remove from the heat.

5. Carefully but quickly, pour the panna cotta into the prepared pan, filling each well three-fourths full. (If using the donut pan, fill all six wells. If using a muffin tin, fill seven or eight wells.)

6. Cover the pan with plastic wrap and place in the refrigerator until the panna cottas are set, 1 to 2 hours.

7. Remove the panna cottas from the refrigerator. Using a thin butter knife, carefully release them from the pan.

8. Splatter or spoon the coulis onto dessert plates. Place a panna cotta on top, and dress with additional coulis. Garnish with an edible flower and a few wineberries before serving.

MAKES 6 SERVINGS

Special equipment: Donut pan or twelve-well muffin tin

Plant-based butter (such as Country Crock avocado oil) or dairy butter, for the pan

Wineberry Coulis

1½ cups wineberries

½ cup pure cane sugar

2 tablespoons water

2 tablespoons triple sec orange liqueur (such as Cointreau)

Panna Cotta

1½ cups coconut cream

3½ ounces white chocolate, chopped, or ¾ cup white chocolate chips

¾ cup plus 1 tablespoon plant-based milk (such as Oatly) or dairy milk

¼ cup plus 1 tablespoon pure cane sugar

1 tablespoon agar powder

1 teaspoon vanilla extract

Edible flowers (such as rose or nasturtium) and wineberries for garnishing

PEACH WINEBERRY SORBET

Sorbets are fun and simple to make. All you really need is frozen fruit, sugar, and a food processor! This peach wineberry sorbet is light, refreshing, and perfect for a hot summer day. The flavors are reminiscent of peach melba, a peach and raspberry dessert. This sorbet has a complex flavor, thanks to the boozy amaretto and almond extract, an overlooked and underutilized ingredient. Everyone will think you're a culinary genius. Using frozen peaches and wineberries means you can skip the freezer and enjoy the sorbet immediately, if desired. To prepare the wineberries, arrange them in a single layer on a baking sheet and freeze until solid, about 3 hours.

MAKES 8 TO 10 SERVINGS

Special equipment: 8 by 4-inch or 9 by 5-inch metal loaf pan

4 cups frozen sliced peaches

2 cups frozen wineberries

1½ cups pure cane sugar

Juice of 1 Meyer lemon

2 tablespoons amaretto liqueur

1 teaspoon almond extract

1. Line a metal loaf pan with parchment paper.

2. In a food processor, combine the peaches, wineberries, sugar, lemon juice, amaretto, and almond extract and puree until very smooth, scraping down the sides as needed.

3. Pour the puree into the prepared pan. Lay a sheet of plastic wrap directly over the surface of the puree, making sure little air can get through.

4. Place the sorbet in the freezer for at least 4 hours (it's ready to serve when it is firm enough to scoop) or up to 1 month.

WILD BLACKBERRIES
(RUBUS PLICATUS)

When I went out to collect these little deep-purple treasures as a child, I'd return home all scratched up, with stained fingers. I would often collect the berries, mash them, and use the juice to paint pictures. I had plenty of art supplies, but my tiny creative mind was always thinking outside the box. Blackberry brambles are beautiful, with the juiciest of berries. They look similar to many other *Rubus* species, which are all edible, including dewberries and black raspberries, which typically grow a bit lower to the ground. Like wineberries, you'll want to collect these wild blackberries in a solid container, so the delicate berries do not burst.

Appearance: Oval, toothed leaflets, which are green on top and silvery white underneath. Prickly, cane-shaped stems. Grow in tall thickets. Flowers are up to 2.5 cm in diameter with five white petals. Many small, fleshy one-seeded fruits make up the entire berry, which is 2 to 2.5 cm long. Berries transition from white to red as they mature, and are deep blackish purple when completely ripe. Berries don't ripen all at once. You can find various stages on the same plant during harvest season.

Smell: Subtly sweet, slightly tart, fragrant.

Taste: Juicy, sweet, more complex than store-bought cultivated berries.

Habitat: Grow in sun or partial shade and are often found along woodland edges.

Region: Across most of North America and are abundant in the Pacific Northwest and eastern United States.

Growth Cycle: Perennial, with seeds present from late summer into fall.

Prime Harvest Season: Late summer.

Dangerous Lookalikes: None.

Fun fact: Blackberries are aggregate fruits composed of multiple smaller individual berries, known as drupelets. Each drupelet contains a seed surrounded by a small amount of pulp. When you eat a blackberry, you're actually consuming a cluster of drupelets that have grown together!

PULLED JACKFRUIT SLIDERS WITH BLACKBERRY BARBECUE SAUCE

Don't know what to bring to the cookout this summer? Try these blackberry barbecue sliders! I love the deep-purple hue and tart edge that the blackberries provide. Pulled jackfruit is simmered in this smoky, sweet sauce and served with arugula on slider buns. This is one of my favorite ways to give blackberries their moment!

MAKES 4 TO 6 SERVINGS

Blackberry Barbecue Sauce

1 cup fresh blackberries, mashed with a fork

2 canned chipotle chiles, chopped, plus 2 tablespoons of the adobo sauce

½ cup ketchup

¼ cup dark brown sugar

¼ cup apple cider vinegar

2 tablespoons water or vegetable stock

2 garlic cloves, minced

1 teaspoon Dijon mustard

½ teaspoon smoked paprika

½ teaspoon ground cumin

1 teaspoon kosher salt

½ teaspoon black pepper

2 tablespoons olive oil

One 14-ounce can young green jackfruit in brine, drained, rinsed, and shredded

½ teaspoon liquid smoke

Quick Slaw

1 cup shredded red cabbage

¼ cup plant-based mayonnaise (such as Hellmann's vegan dressing) or regular mayonnaise

1 tablespoon chopped fresh cilantro

Juice of 1 lime

1 teaspoon neutral oil (such as canola oil or avocado oil)

1 teaspoon pure cane sugar

10 slider buns

¼ small red onion, thinly sliced

1½ cups loosely packed arugula

1. To make the barbecue sauce: In a small saucepan over medium heat, combine the blackberries, chipotles and adobo, ketchup, brown sugar, vinegar, water, garlic, mustard, paprika, cumin, salt, and pepper; stir to incorporate; and bring to a boil. Turn the heat to medium-low and cook, stirring occasionally, until the sauce is thickened, 8 to 10 minutes. Remove from the heat and set aside.

2. In a medium saucepan over medium-low heat, warm the olive oil until it shimmers. Add the jackfruit and liquid smoke and sauté for 2 minutes. Add 1 cup of the barbecue sauce, cover the pan, and turn the heat to low. Let simmer for 5 minutes.

3. To make the slaw: Meanwhile, in a small bowl, combine the cabbage, mayonnaise, cilantro, lime juice, neutral oil, and sugar and mix well.

4. Layer the pulled jackfruit over the bottoms of the slider buns, followed by the slaw, red onions, and arugula. Close the buns and serve immediately.

Basil's potential for brightening a dessert is totally underrated. It is one of my favorite herbs, especially in its summer prime. With undertones of pepper and mint, it plays well with so many ingredients, especially blackberries. The texture of this cobbler is delightful. You experience jammy blackberries, fluffy-yet-dense cake, and crunchy sugar on top. It's not overly sweet, and it impressed my partner, Levon, who is almost never interested in sweets.

BLACKBERRY BASIL COBBLER

1. Preheat the oven to 350°F. Butter the baking dish.

2. In the bottom of the baking dish, combine 1½ cups of the blackberries, the 3 tablespoons cane sugar, and lemon juice. Using the back of a large spoon, lightly mash the berries, being sure to leave most of them in chunks.

3. In a medium bowl, combine the remaining 1 cup cane sugar, flour, baking powder, flaxseed, cinnamon, and salt and whisk to incorporate.

4. In a small bowl, combine the milk and melted butter, whisk to incorporate, and then fold into the dry mixture. Stir well, until the batter is smooth.

5. Using a rubber spatula, fold the remaining 1 cup blackberries and the basil into the batter. Pour the batter evenly over the mashed blackberries in the baking dish, then cover with aluminum foil.

6. Bake the cobbler until the surface is evenly golden brown, 60 to 70 minutes. Remove the foil and bake until the top is slightly crispy, about 5 minutes more. Sprinkle with the turbinado sugar and garnish with basil.

7. Serve the cobbler warm, with a scoop of ice cream.

MAKES 6 TO 8 SERVINGS

Special equipment: 8-inch baking dish

Butter, for the baking dish

2½ cups fresh blackberries

3 tablespoons pure cane sugar, plus 1 cup

Juice of 2 lemons

2 cups all-purpose flour

1 tablespoon baking powder

1 tablespoon ground flaxseed

1 teaspoon ground cinnamon

¼ teaspoon kosher salt

1 cup plant-based milk (such as Oatly) or dairy milk

½ cup plant-based butter (such as Country Crock avocado oil) or dairy butter, melted

½ cup torn fresh basil, plus more for garnishing

2 tablespoons turbinado sugar

Vanilla ice cream for serving

WILD BLUEBERRIES
(VACCINIUM ANGUSTIFOLIUM)

I had the absolute pleasure of visiting the ten-thousand-year-old wild blueberry barrens in Maine for a tour with the Wild Blueberry Association of North America, and my mind was blown. What I thought I knew about these wild berries was nothing compared to the knowledge that I gained from those in the association and the Passamaquoddy Native Americans who still take care of the land. I even had the chance to harvest the blueberries myself, using a hand rake. It was magical.

Wild blueberries are one of the few fruits that are native to North America. They grow in a two-year cycle, which enables vegetative restoration during rest periods. Glacial ice and natural fires produced the right quality and acidity of soil required for blueberries to flourish. Maine wild blueberries are some of the best blueberries I've ever had. There are multiple varieties, which differ in degree of tartness, size, and color. The wild berries are bluer than any blueberry I have ever seen. Boasting twice the number of antioxidants than cultivated berries, this superfood is not only delicious but also extremely nutritious. All the blueberries that we know and love today, whether wild or cultivated, come from berries originally scattered by birds that traveled through Maine. There are two types of blueberries: lowbush and highbush. True wild blueberries only grow in Maine and Canada and are all lowbush. Where I live in Connecticut, highbush blueberries, which are all products of cultivated berries, grow abundantly. To harvest, pick the berries one by one or use a hand rake, and bring a container for gathering your berries so they don't get squished.

Off the grid! Hand raking blueberries in northern Maine with the Wild Blueberry Association of North America.

Appearance: Lowbush berries are small, with ovate, alternately arranged leaves. Leaves are short stalked to nearly stalked, and their hues range from red to yellow to green. Small white or pink flowers grow in clusters in a bell shape. Berries are round and dark blue in color, with a slightly white sheen or coating and a five-pointed crown on one end. Highbush varieties can grow up to 12 feet; have larger berries, lighter in color than lowbush and produce more fruit.

Smell: Mostly indistinct, but fruity and herbaceous when a scent is present.

Taste: Intense blueberry flavor, deeper and more complex than cultivated berries; some varietals are sweeter, others more tart.

Habitat: Acid-rich, dry soil. Typically grow alongside conifers, sometimes grow in pine barrens and mountains.

Region: New England, especially Maine; eastern Canada.

Growth Cycle: Two-year growth cycle.

Prime Harvest Season: July and August.

Dangerous Lookalikes: Nightshade. A shrub-like plant with vine-like branches and arrow-shaped leaves.

Wild blueberries are still considered a bit of a scientific anomaly. Research into wild blueberries and their unique properties and potential health benefits continues to receive funding. They are of interest to scientists due to the genetic diversity of wild blueberry populations. They're known for being rich in antioxidants, vitamins, and other bioactive compounds that have been linked to various health-promoting effects, such as reducing inflammation.

One of my go-to brunch spots in Connecticut is a restaurant named Barcelona. They make incredible olive oil pancakes, which inspired this version. The intense wild blueberry flavor makes these pancakes shine, and the olive oil makes them a little more healthful than conventional recipes. The pancakes come together in fewer than 15 minutes, and they are filled with juicy bursts of flavor. The coolest part of this recipe is the use of aquafaba, the water in which chickpeas have been cooked and canned. It works as a substitute for egg whites and gives the pancakes a fluffy texture. Add this recipe to your Sunday brunch rotation!

WILD BLUEBERRY AND LEMON OLIVE OIL PANCAKES

1. In a small bowl, combine the milk, applesauce, olive oil, and lemon juice and stir to incorporate. In a medium bowl, sift together the flour, baking powder, and baking soda. Add the cane sugar, lemon zest, and salt and whisk to incorporate. Add the wet ingredients to the dry ingredients and whisk into a well combined and smooth batter.

2. Using a fork, whip the aquafaba until foamy and then, using a rubber spatula, fold it into the batter. Fold in the blueberries until well incorporated, making sure not to overmix.

3. In a large skillet over medium-high heat, melt 1 tablespoon of the butter. Add ¼ cup of the batter for each pancake (I personally never cook more than two pancakes at a time) and cook until bubbles form on the surface and the edges of the pancake are dry, 2 to 3 minutes. Using a spatula, flip them and cook for 2 to 3 minutes more, adding butter to the pan as needed. Transfer to a plate, and repeat until you've cooked all the pancakes.

4. Garnish the pancakes with confectioners' sugar, and serve hot with maple syrup.

COOK'S NOTE

The easiest way to get aquafaba is to use the liquid from a can of chickpeas.

MAKES 4 TO 6 SERVINGS

1 cup plant-based milk (such as Oatly) or dairy milk

¼ cup unsweetened applesauce

¼ cup olive oil

Grated zest and juice of 1 lemon

1½ cups all-purpose flour

2 teaspoons baking powder

½ teaspoon baking soda

2 tablespoons pure cane sugar

½ teaspoon kosher salt

2 tablespoons aquafaba (see Cook's Note)

1½ cups fresh blueberries

¼ cup butter or neutral oil (such as canola oil or avocado oil)

Confectioners' sugar for garnishing

Maple syrup for serving

WILD BLUEBERRY SCONES

These scones used to sell out very quickly at an awesome shop I used to make baked goods for called Source Coffeehouse. Many customers would message me on Instagram to tell me how much they enjoyed them. I'd often get comments like, "Wow! These are vegan?" The enthusiastic responses delighted me, as it took a lot of time and experimentation to get these just right. Wild blueberries are only in season for a short time each year, but the great news is that you can always buy them frozen. Wyman's are the best; try them if you don't have fresh berries. An advantage of frozen berries is that when you mix them into the batter, you don't have to worry about bursting the berries prematurely. I hope you love these as much as I do!

MAKES 8 SCONES

Special equipment: Bench scraper, pastry brush

¾ cup oat milk (such as Oatly) or dairy milk

1 teaspoon vanilla extract

½ teaspoon almond extract

2¼ cups all-purpose flour, or as needed

½ cup pure cane sugar

1 tablespoon baking powder

1 tablespoon ground flaxseed

½ teaspoon kosher salt

Grated zest of 1 lemon

½ cup plant-based butter (such as Country Crock avocado oil) or dairy butter, cold and cubed

1 cup wild blueberries, fresh or frozen (do not thaw)

1 tablespoon plant-based heavy whipping cream (such as Silk) or dairy heavy whipping cream

1 tablespoon maple syrup

1 tablespoon turbinado sugar

Vanilla Glaze

¾ cup confectioners' sugar

Juice of ½ lemon

1 tablespoon plant-based heavy whipping cream (such as Silk) or dairy heavy whipping cream

1 teaspoon vanilla extract

1. Preheat the oven to 400°F. Line a baking sheet with parchment paper.

2. In a small bowl, combine the oat milk, vanilla, and almond extract and mix to incorporate. Set aside.

3. In a large bowl, combine the flour, cane sugar, baking powder, flaxseed, salt, and lemon zest and whisk to incorporate. Using your fingers, work the butter into the dry ingredients until large coarse crumbs are formed. Using a rubber spatula, slowly stir in the wet ingredients until a loose dough comes together.

4. Add blueberries to the dough and continue mixing until it forms a nice, cohesive ball. If the dough is too wet, add more flour, 1½ teaspoons at a time, until it is tacky.

5. Lightly flour a work surface. Place the dough on the prepared work surface, and flatten it into a circle, about 1 inch thick. Using a bench scraper, cut the circle into eight equal triangles. Place the dough pieces on the prepared baking sheet, spacing the scones about 2 inches apart.

6. In a small dish, stir together the cream and maple syrup. Using a pastry brush, brush the top of each scone with some of the mixture and then dust with the turbinado sugar.

7. Bake the scones until the tops are golden and lightly cracked, 20 to 25 minutes. Transfer to a wire rack and let cool for 30 minutes.

8. To make the glaze: Meanwhile, in a small bowl, combine the confectioners' sugar, lemon juice, cream, and vanilla and whisk to incorporate.

9. Using the whisk, drizzle the glaze over the scones and let set for about 3 minutes before serving.

This sangria is fruity, fun, and the finest end-of-summer beverage you could ask for. It utilizes several of the summer berries you've learned to forage, with an orange and an apple as well. Make it alcohol-free by swapping out the wine for a nonalcoholic substitute, such as Lussory Tempranillo or Surely Non-Alcoholic red wine, or simply use grape juice. For the Grand Marnier and cognac, substitute orange juice.

WILD BERRY SANGRIA

1. In the large pitcher, combine the blueberries, blackberries, and wineberries and, using a long spoon, gently mash to help macerate, but keep most of them whole. Add the apple, orange, brown sugar, Chianti, Grand Marnier, cognac, mint, and cinnamon to the pitcher. Using the spoon, gently mix so the ingredients are well blended.

2. Cover the pitcher with plastic wrap, transfer to the refrigerator, and let rest overnight to infuse all the flavors.

3. Serve the sangria in tall glasses over ice.

MAKES 12 TO 16 SERVINGS

Special equipment: 1 large, wide-mouth pitcher

1½ cups fresh blueberries

1½ cup fresh blackberries

1½ cup fresh wineberries

1 Honeycrisp apple, peeled and finely chopped

1 medium orange, thinly sliced

¼ cup light brown sugar

One 750ml bottle Chianti, Tempranillo, or Zinfandel

1 cup Grand Marnier liqueur

½ cup cognac (such as Martell)

10 mint sprigs

1 teaspoon ground cinnamon

Ice cubes for serving

STAGHORN SUMAC
(RHUS TYPHINA)

Sumac is a beautiful, towering plant that looks tropical and is part of the cashew family. It has tangy berries with a citrus-like flavor that work well as a lemon replacement. Both the berries and the shoots of the fruit are edible, making sumac highly desirable to many foragers. You've likely seen staghorn sumac, as it often lines the edges of highways. The berries are visible all year-round, although not always prime for foraging. I really love using sumac in lemonade, or as a spice. Its flavor is unique and bright. To harvest, use a foraging knife or kitchen shears to snip the conical cluster of berries from the base. I personally prefer to collect them in a wicker foraging basket, or any sturdy container, so that they do not get crushed. When choosing sumac cones to harvest, pluck a berry off a cone and taste it to see whether it's sour enough or perhaps too sour for you. I prefer the more-sour berries, as they have an intense citrus punch. Different shrubs in the same area may ripen at different times. Beware of staghorn sumac's poisonous look-alike, poison sumac.

Appearance: Rusty red in color, with upright fruit cones, or berry clusters (drupes). Leaves are pointy and divided, with toothed margins. Small yellow-green flowers precede berries. Berries are about 0.3 cm in diameter. Fuzzy twigs are present when berries are ready to harvest.

Smell: Strong lemon scent when leaves or twigs are bruised or crushed.

Taste: Lemony. Intensely tart and tangy with notes of cherry; floral and slightly sweet.

Habitat: Can be found on the edges of meadows and other open areas, and frequently alongside highways and heavily trafficked roads. Prefer full sun.

Region: Native to North America, it grows throughout the United States and Canada.

Growth Cycle: Perennial, with seeds present from late summer into fall.

Prime Harvest Season: Mid- to late summer, although you can harvest through the fall if the berries are sour enough.

Dangerous Lookalikes: Poison sumac. To avoid, do not harvest any species resembling sumac that grows in swampy or boggy areas, as these are not habitats that staghorn sumac likes.

MASSAGED KALE WITH SUMAC-ROASTED ALMONDS

You might have noticed that there aren't that many salad recipes in this book. And there's a reason. Since I was young, I've struggled with various stomach issues. Later in life, I learned that I had a chronic stomach condition that could best be controlled by avoiding raw vegetables altogether, or by eating minimal amounts. That changed the way I approached food entirely because I personally *love* salads. There are very few ways I can enjoy a good one these days, but massaged kale is an option. When you massage kale, it makes the vegetable less bitter and breaks down the fibrous texture, making it easier to digest than other vegetables. The sumac-roasted almonds add the perfect amount of sour, a zing unlike any other (they're also fantastic for snacking). This recipe is clean, simple, protein rich, and makes you feel good. Please note, to make the sumac spice, you'll need at least two weeks of prep time, so planning ahead is essential.

MAKES 6 TO 8 SERVINGS

Sumac-Roasted Almonds

2 bunches sumac berries

1 cup almonds

1 tablespoon olive oil

1 teaspoon kosher salt

½ teaspoon garlic powder

Dijon Dressing

½ cup olive oil

⅓ cup champagne vinegar

¼ cup maple syrup

2 tablespoons Dijon mustard

1 teaspoon onion powder

½ teaspoon garlic powder

½ teaspoon kosher salt

2 cups lacinato kale, roughly chopped

2 cups red kale, roughly chopped

2 tablespoons olive oil (see Cook's Note)

1 medium Honeycrisp apple, thinly sliced

½ medium Granny Smith apple, thinly sliced

1 cup dried cranberries

Freshly ground black pepper

1. To make the roasted almonds: Place the sumac bunches in a medium bowl, leave uncovered, and set in cool, dark, dry place for 2 weeks to dry; I typically put mine in a kitchen cabinet. After 2 weeks, separate the berries from the stalk. Using a mortar and pestle, mash the berries into a fine powder. (Alternatively, grind the sumac berries in a clean coffee or spice grinder.) Sift the berries through a fine-mesh sieve into a small bowl. The red powder is the sumac spice. (Transfer to an airtight container and store at room temperature indefinitely.) Measure 2 tablespoons of the sumac spice into a medium bowl.

2. Preheat the oven to 350°F. Line a baking sheet with parchment paper.

3. Add the almonds, olive oil, salt, and garlic powder to the sumac and stir to combine. Place the spiced almonds on the prepared baking sheet. Bake the almonds for 20 minutes, stirring halfway, then remove from the oven and let cool for 5 minutes.

4. To make the dressing: Meanwhile, in a small bowl, combine the olive oil, vinegar, maple syrup, mustard, onion powder, garlic powder, and salt and whisk to incorporate. Set aside.

5. In a large bowl, combine the lacinato kale, red kale, and olive oil and massage for 3 minutes. The kale will wilt dramatically when properly massaged. Add both apples, the cranberries, and roasted almonds to the kale. Drizzle with the dressing and toss to combine.

6. Garnish the salad with a few grinds of black pepper and enjoy!

COOK'S NOTE

It may seem like this isn't enough olive oil. Trust me when I say it's plenty!

I find that sumac is best when infused slowly into a liquid. The taste and hue of the liquid transforms, becoming more flavorful and deeply colored. In this recipe, sumac is cooked down with strawberries, then strained and mixed with fresh lemon juice, water, and ice. If you have the time, you can slowly infuse the sumac in 1 cup of cold water in the sun using the "sun tea" method to get the best tasting sumac lemonade possible! Simple, refreshing, and deliciously sour!

STRAWBERRY SUMAC LEMONADE

1. Gently rinse the sumac berries under running water.

2. In a small saucepan over low heat, combine 1 cup of the water, the sumac berries, and sugar, stirring to mix. Be sure to keep the heat on low the entire time and the mixture at a very gentle simmer. If it begins to boil rapidly, reduce the heat immediately, as overheating sumac brings out the bitter tannins in the berries.

3. When the sugar has dissolved and the water turns vibrant red, about 5 minutes, remove the mixture from the heat and let cool for 10 minutes. Strain and discard the berries.

4. Transfer the sumac liquid to a blender; add the strawberries, lemon juice, 1 cup of water, and 1 cup of ice; and blend on high speed until bright pink and mostly smooth with a few strawberry seeds, about 2 minutes. Strain the lemonade into a large pitcher. Taste and adjust the sweetness by adding more sugar, if desired.

5. Serve the lemonade in tall glasses over ice.

MAKES 4 SERVINGS

Berries of 2 bunches sumac

2 cups filtered water

¾ cup pure cane sugar, or as needed

1 cup hulled strawberries

Juice of 4 lemons

Ice cubes for serving

WILD MINT
(MENTHA ARVENSIS)

Where I live, wild mint grows abundantly. You can smell the aroma filling the air from a mile away! The wild mint that I usually find is called "apple mint," which boasts fuzzy leaves and typically has a stronger flavor than cultivated mint. Wild mint has the same culinary uses as the cultivated variety and varies in flavor from one of the nineteen species to the next. I've used wild mint for mojitos, to make an extract, and more. It is easy to identify, due to its unmistakable aroma. If you believe you've found mint, crush a leaf between your fingers and take a whiff. If there is a strong minty aroma, use it! To gather, collect the leaves in a bag, or, using shears, cut the last 3 to 8 inches of a stem that is full of leaves. You can use the stems for teas and extracts, as they are edible too.

This variety is known as "apple mint" (*Mentha suaveolens*) or "wooly mint" due to the fuzzy texture of its leaves, which are velvety to the touch. This varietal has a pleasing applelike fragrance and flavor.

Appearance: Comes in varying hues, from light to deep green. All varieties possess square stems and opposite, toothed leaves. Plants grow 6 to 24 inches tall and have tiny white to pink, and sometimes purple, flowers, which often grow at tips of plants. Tends to grow in large colonies.

Smell: Minty, sharp, herbaceous.

Taste: Some species have similar flavor to cultivated mint varieties, others are more nuanced, herbaceous, and fruity.

Habitat: Often thrives in disturbed soils. Prefers moist soil and full to partial sun.

Region: Native to North America, it grows across the United States and Canada.

Growth Cycle: Perennial, grows back each year.

Prime Harvest Season: Spring and summer in New England and the Pacific Northwest, year-round in California.

Dangerous Lookalikes: None.

I used to be intimidated by the word *extract*. I thought it meant I'd have to perform a long process, using a ton of unique ingredients to get it just right. I quickly learned that most extracts are composed of just a very high-alcohol liquor, like grain alcohol, and whatever food is desired as an enhanced flavor—in this case, wild mint. Wild mint is a bit more nuanced and complex than regular mint. Apple mint, for example, has slight undertones of apple. Although it has less mint flavor compared to cultivated varieties, in this extract, its flavor is wildly enhanced, making a great base for desserts, cocktails, and more. I like to preserve my extracts in small dropper bottles after the extract is ready. This way, I can add a very small amount with more precision and control. Add any elements you think might infuse well with mint here—a vanilla bean or an apple make excellent additions. The possibilities are endless. These make great gifts for the special people in your life!

WILD MINT EXTRACT

1. Clap the mint between your palms to help release some of the natural oils in the leaves. You want them to be bruised for optimal flavor.

2. Place the mint in the 1-pint mason jar and add the alcohol, completely submerging the mint.

3. Give the jar a good shake and cover with a lid. Store in a cool, dark place for 1 month, giving the extract a shake once a week.

4. After a month, taste the extract. If it is to your liking, strain the mixture through a fine-mesh sieve, and, using a small funnel, pour the finished extract into the 1-ounce dropper bottles. If it is not to your liking, let sit in the cool, dark place for up to 1 month longer.

5. Store the extract at room temperature for up to 2 years.

MAKES 1 CUP

Special equipment: Sterilized 1-pint mason jar (see page 15), eight 1-ounce dropper bottles

1½ cups fresh mint leaves and stems

1 cup vodka or grain alcohol

I've always been drawn to the flavors of Middle Eastern cuisine, as it's relatively inclusive of alternative diets. This recipe highlights shawarma seasoning, which typically consists of cumin, coriander, and black pepper. Seitan is a high-protein meat substitute made from wheat, and can be found at most grocery stores, but seitan tastes best when made from scratch. This recipe is rich, warm, and bold, and pairs nicely with the cool tzatziki sauce.

SEITAN SHAWARMA CUTLETS WITH TZATZIKI, TOASTED PISTACHIOS & MINT

1. To make the tzatziki: In a medium bowl, combine the cucumber, yogurt, lemon zest and juice, garlic, dill, mint, olive oil, and salt and stir to incorporate. Cover, transfer to the refrigerator, and store for up to 3 days.

2. To make the seitan cutlets: Preheat the oven to 375°F.

3. In a food processor, combine the chickpeas, vegetable stock, mint, tomato paste, lemon juice, vegetable oil, vinegar, shawarma seasoning, onion powder, garlic powder, salt, and black pepper and process until smooth and creamy, 3 to 5 minutes. Add the vital wheat gluten and process until the gluten is warm and tacky to the touch, about 8 minutes more. Let rest in the food processor to let the gluten develop, about 10 minutes. Process the seitan again until it looks stringy, about 5 minutes.

4. Separate the seitan into four pieces and flatten evenly. Place a piece of parsnip in the center of each and wrap the seitan tightly around it on one end, pinching the seitan sealed, and leaving 2 inches of parsnip revealed on the other end. Tightly wrap each seitan cutlet in aluminum foil.

5. Place the foil-wrapped cutlets directly on the oven rack and bake for 1 hour. Remove from the oven and let cool for 15 minutes.

6. On individual plates, make a bed of lettuce and place a seitan cutlet on top. Dollop each cutlet with a large spoonful of tzatziki, and garnish with the pistachios and lemon wheels. Dust with smoked paprika before serving.

MAKES 4 SERVINGS

Tzatziki

1 English cucumber, finely grated

1½ cups plain plant-based yogurt (such as Cocojune or Silk) or dairy yogurt

Grated zest and juice of ½ lemon

2 garlic cloves, grated

1 tablespoon chopped fresh dill

1 tablespoon chopped fresh mint leaves

1 tablespoon olive oil

1 teaspoon kosher salt

Seitan Cutlets

2 cups canned chickpeas, drained and rinsed

1 cup vegetable stock

¼ cup fresh mint leaves, roughly torn

2 tablespoons tomato paste

Juice of ½ lemon

2 tablespoons vegetable oil or olive oil

1 teaspoon apple cider vinegar

1 tablespoon shawarma seasoning

1 tablespoon onion powder

2 teaspoons garlic powder

½ teaspoon kosher salt

¼ teaspoon black pepper

1¾ cups vital wheat gluten

1 large parsnip, quartered lengthwise

Bib lettuce for serving

½ cup pistachios, toasted (see Cook's Note, page 27)

Lemon wheels for garnishing

Smoked paprika for dusting

WILD MINT MOJITOS

This is a peak summer cocktail, so get ready to forage mint to your heart's content! Originating in Cuba, the mojito is a preparation of mint, lime, and sugarcane. My iteration uses turbinado sugar, which captures the caramel undertones of raw sugarcane. Coconut sugar also works well here, so feel free to use what you have on hand. And for a more full-bodied mint flavor, add 1 or 2 drops of Wild Mint Extract (page 175) per glass. When you sit back and drink a mojito, you'll feel transported to a Caribbean island.

MAKES 2 SERVINGS

Special equipment: 2 pint glasses

Mint Simple Syrup

½ cup fresh mint leaves

½ cup turbinado sugar

½ cup water

12 mint fresh leaves

1 lime, cut into wedges, plus 2 lime wheels for garnishing

4 ounces white rum or nonalcoholic white rum (such as Lyre's White Cane)

Ice cubes as needed

8 ounces club soda

1. To make the simple syrup: In a small saucepan over medium-low heat, combine the mint, turbinado sugar, and water. Bring the mixture to a simmer, making sure not to let it boil, or you'll lose some of the flavor of the mint. Turn the heat to low and let simmer until the sugar is dissolved, about 5 minutes. Remove from the heat and let the syrup cool. Strain the mint leaves from the syrup. Set aside 1½ ounces of the cooled syrup and transfer the remaining syrup to a bottle and store in the refrigerator for up to 4 days.

2. Divide the mint leaves and lime wedges between two pint glasses. Using a muddler or wooden spoon, muddle the mint and lime together until they're juicy.

3. Put 2 ounces of rum and ¾ ounce of the simple syrup in each glass and stir to combine with the lime juice and mint. Fill each glass with ice and top it off with 4 ounces of club soda.

4. Garnish each mojito with a lime wheel and enjoy!

03

GREETINGS, FALL

Autumn reminds me that life, too, is seasonal. It's symbolic of beauty, patience, grace, and evolution. The beauty of autumn is admired by all, its iridescence unlike anything else in nature. It's a season that can teach the hardest of hearts the lesson of transformation, of letting go.

The day was crisp, yet inviting. Woodsmoke tickled my nose, and a feeling of warmth filled my body. A gust of wind stung my cheeks, and a faint red color must have peeked through my brown skin, like the tawny oak leaves falling airily to the forest floor. The trees let go of their leaves, one by one, as vibrant yellow-ochre, sunset-orange, deep-purple, and brick-red hues flushed the boscage. The small waterfall, which was dry during the summer drought, sounded its relief as water rushed through the ravine. The crunch of leaves underfoot reminded me that in nature you're never alone. It was a perfect fall day, and everything felt pristine.

I went to the woods that day in hopes of collecting some lingering fall mushrooms. We had plenty of rain during the previous week, so oysters, shrimp of the woods, and more were sure to be abundant. I knew that, although I had dropped mostly everything, I had to continue writing this book. But it wasn't the main reason I was there that day. Everything else was secondary. I went to the woods to seek healing in nature, and to obtain a semblance of peace.

It is my belief that our gifts, our knowledge, and our passions are greater than us. They're meant to be shared, to be used in love, and to help others to have a better understanding of the world around them. This day would be different than any other. I've always used cooking and foraging to bring others joy, but this time, it was to help heal and comfort a very close friend who was suffering.

When I got the news a few weeks prior that my friend Brian was terminally ill, nothing mattered but him. "What can I do?" was all I could think. I knew he was fading fast, but I wanted to help make his last days as comfortable as I possibly could. Venturing into the woods to find anti-inflammatory mushrooms to make him herbal teas—turkey tail, chaga, lion's mane, anything I could get my hands on—was the least I could do. I wanted to give him something to believe in.

After taking in the beauty of nature and all it had to offer, I said "Thank you" out loud, followed by a little prayer. Brian loved nature. He was bedridden, not having had the chance to go outside in weeks. I took out my phone and recorded small videos of my trek in the woods to show him, so he could experience autumn from inside his home. No one believed in me the way he did. Absolutely no one. It made him smile to see that I was continuing my passion, amid all

that was happening. When I was ready to give up on my culinary career back in 2021, he quickly became my reason to continue, and to this day he remains my inspiration.

I felt that his last day could be nearing fast. I didn't think, however, that it would be the day after that magical, hopeful experience I had in the woods. His last words to me were, "I'm so grateful." He squeezed my hand, which I knew took a lot out of him. I've never cried harder, but I know that I have purpose in this world, and that while I am strong and healthy, I have to give this life all that I've got.

During his final week, I provided all the comfort I could, cooking his favorite meals and editing many of the photos in this book by his side, while he lay in a hospital bed. This, I thought to myself, is how you use the gifts you have been bestowed: to enrich the lives of those you love.

Everything has its time. Seasons will change and leaves will continue to fall. It's simply the cycle of life. What lives on is how people, places, and, sometimes, things leave their mark on you and the world around them. You may forget some stories. You may not remember every minute detail. But the one thing you can never forget is the way someone or something made you feel, and I think that's very powerful.

I will always love the fall. It will still be my favorite season. A celestial gem of change, growth, and letting go—sometimes, forever.

PAWPAWS
(ASMINA TRILOBA)

Pawpaws are a delicious fruit, native to North America. They're custard-like in texture and taste like a cross between a banana and a mango. I spent years in search of this fruit and was lucky enough to be invited to a fellow forager's home, where they grew in her backyard. The power of community in the foraging world knows no bounds! Perhaps one of the most interesting facets of pawpaw is that two cultivars must cross-pollinate for the trees to produce fruit. You will know that a pawpaw is ripe when it is soft to the touch when pressed. Please be careful, as only the inner flesh of the pawpaw is edible. Avoid the skin and seeds, as both components are toxic to humans. Gather the fruit by gently shaking the tree. Ripe fruit will fall to the ground. Collect the pawpaws in a shopping bag and eat them within 3 days, as they spoil quickly unless preserved.

Appearance: Trees are grayish brown, slightly stippled bark, similar to gray birch, with raised pores. Maximum height of 40 feet. Alternate leaves are oblong, 6 to 12 inches long, with smooth edges and pointy tips. Fruit is about the size of a small mango. Unripe fruit appears pale-green and gradually turns to yellow-green or all yellow as fruit ripens. Large black seeds line center of fruit. Flesh is yellow to yellow-orange, with a smooth, soft texture when ripe.

Smell: Fruity, floral, banana-like aroma.

Taste: Notes of banana, papaya, mango.

Habitat: Deep, rich fertile soils of river bottomlands, typically in wooded areas. Grow well in full sun or light shade.

Region: Native to North America. Grows primarily on the East Coast; parts of the Midwest, including Indiana; and from Florida north to Ontario, Canada.

Growth Cycle: Annual, with seeds present from late summer into fall.

Prime Harvest Season: Late summer through early fall.

Dangerous Lookalikes: None.

Did you know that pawpaws are the largest edible fruit native to North America? They are often referred to as "custard apples" due to their creamy texture and sweet tropical flavor!

Pawpaw season is short, and the fruit doesn't last long after ripening. That means there is only a short window in which to use all your foraged fruit, which may be daunting. This puree is a good way to preserve the flesh, which you can use in a variety of ways when you're ready. Remember that only the inner flesh is edible and that the skin and seeds are toxic to humans. This recipe can, of course, be multiplied to match the size of your harvest.

PAWPAW PUREE

1. Peel and discard the pawpaws' skin. Scrape all the flesh into a food processor, discarding the black seeds in the center of the fruit. Process until smooth.

2. Vacuum seal the puree or transfer it to ziplock freezer bags. (Alternatively, you can pour the puree into ice-cube trays with covers.)

3. Store the puree in the freezer for up to 3 months.

MAKES 4 CUPS

Special equipment: Vacuum sealer

10 pawpaw fruit

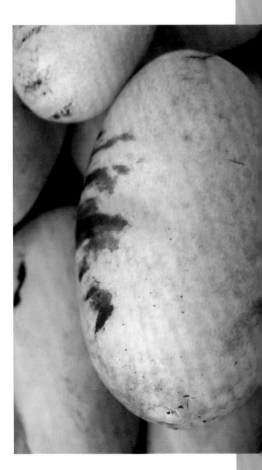

My friends Noelia and Abe are from Puerto Rico, where the delicious tradition of coquito originates. Coquito is a seasonal Puerto Rican beverage with a base of coconut (in different forms), condensed milk, rum, and various spices. *Coquito* literally means "little coconut" in Spanish. Noelia and Abe once gave me a 2-quart mason jar filled with coquito. It was one of the best gifts I have ever received. They had one requirement before sharing the recipe: That I share it with family and friends in the spirit of the holidays. Now I am sharing my version of coquito with you, this time with foraged pawpaws. This recipe is easily scalable, so make as much or as little as you want, and gift it to the ones you love this holiday season.

COQUITO

1. In the high-speed blender, combine the pawpaw puree, coconut cream, coconut milk, evaporated coconut milk, sweetened condensed milk, chai tea, rum, ginger, ground cinnamon, nutmeg, and cardamom. Blend on high speed until the mixture is smooth, and little or no chunks of coconut cream remain, 3 minutes, scraping down the sides of the blender as needed.

2. Pour the coquito into a large pitcher, then stir in the cloves, peppercorns, and cinnamon sticks. Cover, transfer to the refrigerator, and let sit overnight, or up to 24 hours, to allow the flavors to meld and deepen.

3. The coquito will keep in the refrigerator for up to 1 week, but separation might occur. Before serving, give it a good stir to make sure it is homogenous. When serving, avoid solids such as peppercorns and cinnamon sticks.

MAKES 6 TO 8 SERVINGS

Special equipment: High-speed blender

1 cup Pawpaw Puree (page 187)

One 14-ounce can coconut cream

One 14-ounce can coconut milk

One 14-ounce can evaporated coconut milk

One 11¼-ounce can sweetened condensed coconut milk or sweetened condensed oat milk (such as Nature's Charm)

1 cup chai tea, at room temperature

8 ounces white or spiced rum or nonalcoholic rum (such as Ritual Zero Proof or Lyre's)

One 1-inch piece ginger, peeled and grated

1 teaspoon ground cinnamon

½ teaspoon ground nutmeg

Seeds of 5 cardamom pods

12 whole cloves

12 black peppercorns

3 cinnamon sticks

MATSUTAKE
(TRICHOLOMA MATSUTAKE)

The first time I came across matsutake, I was with my foraging mentor, Chris, in a city park in Vermont that had hiking trails. The forest was very dense, nutrient rich, and moist, with mixed conifer and oak trees, so I had a feeling it was going to be a good foraging day. One of my favorite things about the forest was that it had streams full of natural soft clay, which looked like rock shelves. Lo and behold, we found an abundance of white matsutake alongside yellow foot chanterelles and black trumpets. It felt too good to be true. The matsutake is an incredible mushroom because it is one of the few that can be eaten raw. The flavor is sharp, rich, and deep, and unlike any other mushroom I have tasted. It is considered a choice edible. To harvest, use a foraging knife to dig up the mushroom from the base, where the stem forms a "pin" in the ground. Begin by loosening the soil around it, and slowly and carefully wiggle the mushroom back and forth until you can remove the entire mushroom without breaking it.

Appearance: Creamy to buff-colored bell-shaped cap; veiled when young, becoming more flattened or slightly depressed at center with age. Dry, scaly texture with short, stout stem; slightly swollen at base.

Cap: Smooth, 5 to 20 cm wide, convex transitioning to flat in shape. From pale buff to dark reddish brown scales and spots. Paler white at the margin. Cottony in texture, slightly tacky when young and ripe, and becoming drier with age.

Underside: Attached gills that are moderately spaced yet somewhat crowded. Whitish; stains pinkish brown when cut. Veiled.

Stalk: Cylindrical, solid. From 5 to 15 cm long, 2 to 4 cm thick, tapering toward base. At its prime, sheathed from base to ring by soft white veil.

Spore Print: Spores are released from the gills and create a white spore print.

Smell: Pungent, damp-forest, sometimes cinnamon-like, spicy, and sweet.

Flavor Profile: Complex, earthy, aromatic. Sometimes spicy to peppery.

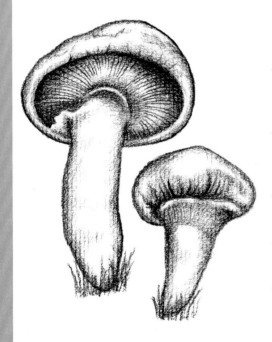

Habitat: Present in conifer forests and in sandy soil of coastal areas. Particularly mossy forest floors alongside various conifer species such as spruce, hemlock, and other pine species. Prefer well-drained, acidic soil.

Region: Northeastern United States, through the Pacific Northwest, and Canada.

Prime Harvest Season: August to November in most of North America, and December to February in California.

Dangerous Lookalikes: Smith's amanita. A large, white mushroom with wart-like patches on the cap; a torn ring on a scaly, rooting stem that is slightly bulbous (like matsutake); brittle texture; and an unpleasant chemical/decaying protein scent. Common in the Pacific Northwest and Northern California.

ROASTED BERBERE SPICED BUTTERNUT SQUASH WITH **SHAVED MATSUTAKE**

Matsutake is one of the most flavorful mushrooms I have ever come across. They're spicy, pungent, and piney, and they pair well with berbere seasoning and roasted butternut squash. The squash gets poked and scored to ensure there is flavor in every inch, and the crispy edges are one of the best parts of this dish. Berbere seasoning is a delicious spicy mix of dried spices used in Ethiopian cuisine. I love it because it reminds me of Jamaican jerk seasoning. Look for it in the international or spice aisle of your supermarket.

MAKES 4 TO 6 SERVINGS

1 large butternut squash, halved and seeded

1 tablespoon berbere seasoning

1 teaspoon smoked paprika

1 teaspoon kosher salt

½ teaspoon black pepper

3 tablespoons avocado oil

2 tablespoons maple syrup

2 tablespoons plant-based butter (such as Country Crock avocado oil) or dairy butter, melted

½ cup grated or thinly sliced matsutake mushroom

Chopped fresh parsley and pomegranate seeds for garnishing

Flaky sea salt

1. Preheat the oven to 450°F. Line a baking sheet with parchment paper.

2. Using the tip of a sharp knife, make horizontal and vertical slits about ½ inch deep all over the cut side of the squash.

3. In a small dish, combine the berbere seasoning, smoked paprika, kosher salt, and black pepper and stir to incorporate.

4. Sprinkle the spices generously over the surface of the squash flesh, and try to get some of the seasoning into the slits. Drizzle the avocado oil evenly over the squash, followed by the maple syrup. Place the squash cut-side up on the prepared baking sheet.

5. Bake the squash until the flesh is soft and golden brown, about 40 minutes. Remove from the oven.

6. Carefully position an oven rack on the center rack, and preheat the broiler.

7. Drizzle the squash with the melted butter and broil until the squash is caramelized with brown edges, has a crisp top layer, and is fork-tender at the center, about 10 minutes. Let the squash cool for 5 minutes.

8. Sprinkle the matsutake over the squash, then garnish with parsley, pomegranate seeds, and sea salt. Enjoy hot.

This dish is stellar. Beet ravioli are filled with my signature almond ricotta and sautéed matsutake, then drizzled with jerk cream sauce for a hint of spice and a taste of Jamaica. The ravioli are easy to make, and the beet puree adds a subtle red tint, as impressive on the palate as it is on the eyes. Although the preparation is time-consuming, you can easily scale it up and freeze the extra dough to make it worth your while.

BEET RAVIOLI WITH SAUTÉED MATSUTAKE & JERK CREAM

1. To make the dough: In a medium pot over medium-high heat, combine the beets and enough water to cover completely and bring to a boil. Turn the heat to medium-low, cover, and simmer until fork-tender, 25 to 40 minutes. Reserve some of the cooking water. In a blender, combine the beets and ¼ cup water and puree on high speed until smooth, adding 1 tablespoon of the cooking water at a time, as needed, about 1 minute. Set aside.

2. In a large bowl, combine the flour, flaxseed, oregano, thyme, and salt. Make a well in the center of the dry ingredients and add the beet puree and olive oil. Using a rubber spatula, stir the dry ingredients into the wet, then, using your hands, knead the dough into a ball. Transfer the dough to a lightly floured surface and knead until smooth, about 3 minutes. Return the dough to the bowl and cover with a damp kitchen towel to let the gluten rest, about 10 minutes.

3. To make the filling: Meanwhile, in a small saucepan over medium heat, warm the olive oil until it shimmers. Add the matsutake, champagne vinegar, salt, and black pepper and stir to combine. Sauté the matsutake until silky, about 2 minutes, then remove from the heat. Stir in the almond ricotta and set aside.

4. Bring a large pot of water to a boil. Divide the dough into two even pieces. On a clean work surface, roll each piece into a 6 by 8-inch rectangle; set one aside on a sheet of parchment paper. Using a knife or pastry cutter, mark the dough on your work surface into six equal sections. Fill the center of each one with 1 tablespoon of the filling then sprinkle with chives. Place the second sheet of dough on top of the filled layer, gently pressing down around each filled center with your fingers. Using a pasta cutter, cut the ravioli into six pieces, removing any excess dough. Set aside.

5. To make the sauce: In a small saucepan over medium heat, melt the butter. Add the flour and stir vigorously until smooth and bubbly, 1 to 2 minutes. Turn the heat to low, whisk in the jerk seasoning and sugar, and cook for 1 minute. Whisk in the almond milk; the sauce should be silky, yet thick enough to drizzle.

6. Add the ravioli to the boiling water and cook until they float to the top, about 3 minutes. Plate the ravioli, drizzle with the jerk cream, and garnish with chives and red pepper flakes.

MAKES 4 TO 6 SERVINGS

Special equipment: High-speed blender, pasta cutter

Beet Ravioli Dough

2 medium beets, peeled and ends trimmed

¼ cup water

2 cups all-purpose flour, plus more for the work surface

2 tablespoons flaxseed

1 teaspoon dried oregano

½ teaspoon dried thyme

½ teaspoon kosher salt

2 tablespoons olive oil

Filling

1 tablespoon olive oil

½ cup finely diced matsutake mushroom

1 teaspoon champagne vinegar

¼ teaspoon kosher salt

¼ teaspoon black pepper

1 cup almond ricotta (see page 98)

1 cup chopped chives

Jerk Cream Sauce

¼ cup plant-based butter (such as Country Crock avocado oil) or dairy butter

2 tablespoons all-purpose flour

2 teaspoons jerk seasoning

1 teaspoon pure cane sugar

2 tablespoons unsweetened almond milk, at room temperature

Chopped chives and red pepper flakes for garnishing

CRABAPPLES
(MALUS)

There are thirty-five unique species of crabapple, and an incredible seven hundred cultivated varieties of crabapple trees. They are native to North America and Asia and are commonly grown in the United States as an ornamental tree. So finding a tree while urban foraging is highly likely! When I was growing up, my neighbors on our cul-de-sac had a big crabapple tree in their yard. It produced rather large fruit, the size of a small, cultivated apple, which isn't always the case with crabapples. I remember trying the fruit as a kid, and, oh, how I disliked them back then! I didn't realize that not every apple on a crabapple tree is sour. For crabapples to taste their best, they require a frost—the cold temperature makes the fruit sweeter. They're best cooked, as they are typically very tart when raw, and they make for great jellies due to their natural pectin content. Be sure to harvest the apples carefully, so you don't strip bark off the tree.

Did you know that crabapples were once used as the primary source of pectin for making jellies and jams?

Appearance: Vary in color from shades of yellow to greens and reds. Size ranges from as small as a pea to a golf ball, sometimes a little larger, with five seeds in fruit's center in a pentacle pattern. Beautiful five-petaled pink and white flowers bloom in clusters on long grouped stems in April or May.

Smell: Fruity and floral.

Taste: Most varieties are tart to very tart, others are slightly sweet.

Habitat: Woods, roadsides, and forest edges. Also found in oak forests with good air circulation. Grows best in moist, well-drained soils in full sun to partial shade.

Region: Throughout North America, especially in temperate climates. Native to regions of Asia, Europe, and North America.

Growth Cycle: Annual, with seeds present from late summer into fall.

Prime Harvest Season: Best flavor from late fall through winter.

Dangerous Lookalikes: None.

CRABAPPLE CRISPS

When I was growing up, my mom and older sister, Dillian, often made apple crisp. I remember the aroma of sweet cinnamon, brown sugar, and apple filling me with joy. The entire house would smell of apples and spice for hours. Apple crisp is an excellent way to utilize an abundance of crabapples, especially because you don't have to go through the painstaking task of seeding every single fruit. Since each serving is on a smaller scale than most apple crisps, you won't eat enough seeds to get an upset stomach. This recipe will make you feel warm and comforted; I guarantee it.

MAKES 4 SERVINGS

Special equipment: Four 4-inch ramekins

½ cup old fashioned oats

4 tablespoons plant-based butter (such as Country Crock avocado oil) or dairy butter, melted

4 tablespoons brown sugar, plus more for sprinkling

2 tablespoons all-purpose flour

2 teaspoons ground cinnamon

½ teaspoon ground nutmeg

2 cups crabapples, halved

4 scoops vanilla ice cream (optional)

1. Preheat the oven to 350°F. Grease the ramekins with butter or cooking spray.

2. In a medium bowl, combine the oats, 2 tablespoons of the melted butter, 2 tablespoons of the brown sugar, the flour, 1 teaspoon of the cinnamon, and the nutmeg and stir to incorporate.

3. In another medium bowl, combine the crabapples and the remaining 2 tablespoons melted better, 2 tablespoons brown sugar, and 1 teaspoon cinnamon and stir together. Divide evenly among the prepared ramekins and top with the oat mixture.

4. Sprinkle a little more brown sugar on top of each ramekin and then cover with aluminum foil.

5. Bake the crisps for 20 minutes. Remove the foil and continue to bake until the top is golden, about 5 minutes more.

6. Serve the crabapple crisps, warm, with ice cream, if using.

This is my favorite way to prepare crabapples. Pickled crabapples are tangy, juicy, and aromatic. They go well with Thanksgiving roasts and are also good on oatmeal, since they work with sweet or savory dishes. Plus, pickling is the best way to preserve your crabapples, and they can be frozen in a mason jar for use throughout the year. If you're looking for an impressive Thanksgiving side, this recipe is the one!

SPICED PICKLED CRABAPPLES

1. In a medium saucepan over medium-high heat, combine the crabapples, vinegar, water, bourbon, almond extract, cardamom pods, cinnamon sticks, ground cinnamon, brown sugar, allspice, pepper, and salt and stir to incorporate. Bring the mixture to a rolling boil, and gently mash half of the apples in the pan to release their juices.

2. Turn the heat to medium-low and cook, stirring occasionally, until the juice thickens, like a glaze on the whole apples, about 45 minutes. Taste a crabapple. If you want the pickles to be more acidic, add more vinegar; if you prefer them sweeter, add more brown sugar. Let cook for 10 minutes more and then discard the cardamom pods.

3. Add the apples, liquid, and spices to the mason jar, leaving ½ to 1 inch of headspace. Seal the jar and allow the apples to cool to room temperature.

4. Store the pickled crabapples in the refrigerator for up to 1 week, or in the freezer for up to 1 year.

MAKES 1½ CUPS

Special equipment: One sterilized 12-ounce mason jar (see page 15) or an airtight plastic storage container

3 cups whole crabapples

1 cup apple cider vinegar or champagne vinegar, or as needed

½ cup filtered water

3 tablespoons bourbon or whiskey

1 teaspoon almond extract

5 cardamom pods

2 cinnamon sticks

1½ teaspoons ground cinnamon

2 teaspoons dark brown sugar, or as needed

1 teaspoon ground allspice

1 teaspoon black pepper

½ teaspoon kosher salt

LION'S MANE MUSHROOMS
(HERICIUM ERINACEUS)

"Lion's mane" is loosely used to describe many species in the *Hericium* family, but the mushroom it commonly refers to is *Hericium erinaceus*. All *Hericium* species are edible and very similar in flavor, but the species you forage will depend on where you live. All *Hericium* are tooth fungi, which refers to their pure-white flesh and how they grow in small to large masses with toothlike structures. These are choice edible mushrooms. I love their seafood-like texture and flavor, and their versatile cooking possibilities. My favorite thing to make with them is crabcakes. To harvest, cleanly slice your *Hericium* from its host tree, being sure to trim any woody edges before placing in a paper bag.

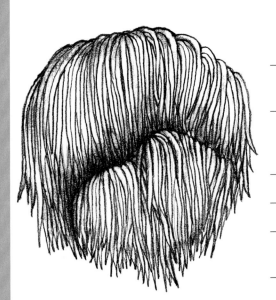

Appearance: Grows in a single beard-like mass, with several long "teeth" (often referred to as spines) that hang from central stalk. Appears shaggy. Stark white to brownish yellow with age. From 10 to 25 cm wide and high. Teeth are 1 to 4 cm long, covering stalk and forming lines rather than tufts.

Stalk: Short, thick. Mostly indistinct, as all teeth grow out from central stalk.

Spore Print: Spore prints are white and released through the basidia (microscopic spore-bearing structures on the surface of the mushroom).

Smell: Fresh and earthy.

Flavor Profile: Nutty, creamy, and mild, with sweet undertones.

Habitat: Typically old oak, maple, and beech tree forests. Tends to grow on older or dying hardwood trees.

Region: Can be found scattered throughout the United States. From the Pacific Northwest to California to Florida, up through New York, Vermont, and Michigan. May be scattered in other regions depending on local environmental conditions.

Prime Harvest Season: Late summer to fall throughout the United States.

Dangerous Lookalikes: None.

Lion's mane is perhaps one of the most unique-looking mushrooms, with long, cascading spines that resemble a lion's mane and give the mushroom its name.

LION'S MANE CRABCAKES WITH **SPICY** GARLIC AIOLI

Lion's mane mushrooms have a fibrous and flaky texture that somewhat resembles the texture of crabmeat when cooked. This makes them an excellent plant-based option for dishes like crabcakes. They're also known for their ability to absorb and take on the flavors of the ingredients they are cooked with. This recipe makes for a fantastic appetizer, and the spicy garlic aioli takes it over the top! Aquafaba, the liquid in canned chickpeas, is used instead of the usual eggs to bind the crabcakes together.

MAKES 12 TO 14 CRABCAKES

Special equipment: Deep-fry/candy thermometer

Garlic Aioli

½ cup plant-based mayonnaise (such as Hellmann's vegan dressing) or regular mayonnaise

2 garlic cloves, grated on a Microplane or minced

2 teaspoon sriracha, or as needed

¼ teaspoon Old Bay seasoning

Crabcakes

2 cups hand-shredded lion's mane mushrooms

½ cup panko bread crumbs

½ cup thinly sliced green onions, white and green parts

Grated zest and juice of 1 lemon

One 4-inch nori sheet, crushed and then cut into tiny pieces or ground in a spice grinder

1 tablespoon minced fresh parsley

1 tablespoon Old Bay seasoning

1 teaspoon kosher salt

½ teaspoon black pepper

¼ teaspoon cayenne pepper

3 tablespoons aquafaba (see headnote)

2 teaspoons Dijon mustard

Neutral oil (such as canola oil or avocado oil) for frying

Dill sprigs for garnishing

Flaky sea salt

Lemon wedges for serving

1. To make the aioli: In a small bowl, combine the mayonnaise, garlic, sriracha, and Old Bay and whisk to incorporate. Taste and add more sriracha if you want the aioli spicier. Set aside.

2. To make the crabcakes: In a large bowl, combine the shredded mushrooms, panko, green onions, lemon zest, nori, parsley, Old Bay, salt, black pepper, and cayenne and stir to blend.

3. In a small bowl, combine the lemon juice, aquafaba, and Dijon mustard and whisk to incorporate.

4. Fold the liquid mixture into the mushroom mixture, and, using your hands, work them together until you have a solid mass. Take ¼ cup of the combined mixture, flatten it between your palms, and place on a plate. Repeat with the remaining mixture.

5. In a large saucepan over medium-high heat, warm ½ inch of neutral oil until it registers 350°F on a deep-fry/candy thermometer. Add the crabcakes, two to four at a time to avoid crowding the pan, and fry until golden and crispy to the touch, 2 to 3 minutes per side. Transfer to paper towels to drain.

6. Place the crabcakes on individual plates and top each with a small dollop of aioli, garnish with a sprig of dill, and sprinkle with flaky salt. Serve with lemon wedges.

This dish may look fancy, but you'll be pleased with how easy it is to create! To make confit, food is cooked in animal fat, oil, or syrup at a low temperature. This ensures the flavors are slowly infused into the food—in this case, the mushroom. Endives are charred in a skillet with a method that I've only seen Chef Jacques Pépin use, caramelizing the outside of the endive in a simple, yet highly appetizing way. The mushrooms and endives are plated over a delicious lemony pea puree, which is incredibly pleasing on the palate, and served with citrus. If you want to make a stunning and highly flavorful dish, this one is for you.

LION'S MANE CONFIT WITH PEA PUREE & CHARRED ENDIVE

1. To make the confit: In a deep medium saucepan over medium heat, combine the olive oil, mushrooms, garlic, chile, shallot, thyme, oregano, bay leaves, and salt and bring to a gentle simmer. Turn the heat to medium-low, cover the pan, and continue to simmer, stirring occasionally, until the mushrooms are slightly crisp and golden brown, and the garlic is soft, 40 to 45 minutes. There should be gentle bubbles present during the entire cooking time. Remove from the heat.

2. To make the puree: While the mushrooms are cooking, in a small skillet (with a lid) over medium-high heat, melt the butter. Add the peas, lemon juice, sugar, and salt and cook, stirring frequently, until the peas are tender, about 5 minutes. Transfer to a high-speed blender and blend on high speed until the peas are pureed. Strain through a sieve set over a bowl, discarding any solids. Set aside.

3. To make the charred endives: Sprinkle the sugar across the bottom of a large skillet and set over medium-high heat. Spread the endives, cut-side down, in the pan in an even layer. Sear for 2 minutes, dribbling in 2 tablespoons of the water. Add the remaining 1 tablespoon water, cover the pan, and cook until the cut sides are slightly charred, golden, and caramelized, 1 to 2 more minutes more. Set aside.

4. Spoon a layer of pea puree onto individual plates, put a mushroom in the center of the pool, and add some of the garlic cloves. Place two endive halves on each serving, and garnish with the citrus.

MAKES 4 SERVING

Special equipment: High-speed blender

Confit

3 cups olive oil

4 small to medium whole lion's mane mushrooms

10 garlic cloves

1 Scotch bonnet chile, or 1 teaspoon red pepper flakes

1 shallot, halved

4 thyme sprigs

3 oregano sprigs

2 bay leaves

1 teaspoon kosher salt

Pea Puree

3 tablespoons plant-based butter (such as Country Crock avocado oil) or dairy butter

1 cup fresh peas

Juice of 1 lemon

1 teaspoon granulated sugar

¼ teaspoon kosher salt

Charred Endive

2 teaspoons granulated sugar

4 endives, halved lengthwise

3 tablespoons water

1 citrus fruit (such as grapefruit or orange), segmented

MAITAKE MUSHROOMS
(GRIFOLA FRONDOSA)

Maitake mushrooms, often referred to as "hen of the woods," are a fantastic fungus for first-time foragers. They have a unique look and are very easy to spot in the woods. The largest maitake mushroom I ever found was twenty pounds! They are one of the most abundant mushrooms, and where you find one, you often find many. Maitake mushrooms are hearty, fleshy, and a choice edible. They're delicious when seared or fried and, boasting a rich flavor profile, can be used in place of chicken. When collecting maitakes, make sure to use a foraging knife to loosen the base of the mushroom. I always put my maitakes in a paper or mesh bag, so that the mushrooms can continue dropping their spores and reproducing. Before taking the mushroom mass home, shake it to get rid of dirt, debris, and any beetles that may be living in it. Maitakes are prime for harvesting when only slightly moist and mostly bug-free, but it is normal to find little beetles hanging out within the mass. If the mushroom you found falls apart too easily, it's best to leave it be. Keep your eyes peeled when looking for this mushroom. Although they are large in size, their coloration sometimes blends with the forest floor!

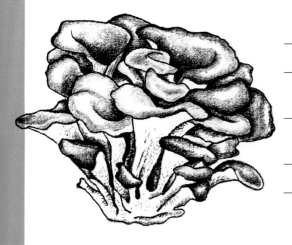

Appearance: Characterized by a distinctive cluster of overlapping, fan-shaped caps making up one large mass; often irregularly shaped, ranging in color from pale to dark brown or gray-brown. The undersides feature a network of whitish to creamy white branching structures.

Cap: When young, pale to light brown, turning dark brown to gray-brown with a blueish tinge with age; less commonly white. Ranging from flat to spoon shaped. From 2 to 7 cm wide and 3 to 5 mm thick. Texture is dry and smooth.

Underside: Many small round whitish to yellowish pores.

Stalk: White and smooth; very short, branched, and indistinct. Often referred to as "fronds."

Spore Print: Spores are released from the pores, and spore prints are white.

Smell: Earthy, woodsy, herbal.

Flavor Profile: Umami, rich, earthy.

Habitat: Often found in oak and maple forests, at base of trees. Sometimes found at base of conifers or on stumps.

Region: East Coast of the United States, southwest to Louisiana. British Columbia, Ontario, Quebec, and Nova Scotia in Canada.

Prime Harvest Season: September to November in northeastern and central United States; October to December in southeastern United States, depending on climate variations and weather factors; August to November in Canada.

Dangerous Lookalikes: None.

LINGUINE WITH SPICY TOMATO BROTH

There is a restaurant named Nico, in Boston's North End, that my partner, Levon, loves. It's a cute little Italian place with great sauces. He often gets a linguine-and-clam dish that is served in a spicy tomato broth. I once tried the broth, and the flavor was exquisite. Levon wanted to be able to make it at home, so I told him I would attempt to "veganize" it first, so that he could have the base recipe and adjust from there. It has been fun to experiment with flavors and textures to try to re-create this dish. The maitake mushrooms replace the clams, while the sauce achieves the spicy, brothy, tomatoey goodness of the original.

MAKES 4 TO 6 SERVINGS

1 pound linguine

4 tablespoons olive oil

½ cup plant-based butter (such as Country Crock avocado oil) or dairy butter

10 garlic cloves

1 tablespoon nori powder, or two 4-inch nori sheets, crushed and then cut into tiny pieces or ground in a spice grinder

1½ teaspoons kosher salt

1½ teaspoons red pepper flakes

1 teaspoon dried oregano

1 teaspoon pure cane sugar

1 teaspoon MSG

1 cup chopped or torn maitake mushrooms (1-inch pieces)

¼ cup tomato paste

2 pints cherry tomatoes

¾ cup dry white vermouth (such as Noilly Prat or Dolin)

1½ cups vegetable broth

1 teaspoon black pepper

Grated zest and juice of 1 lemon

1. Bring a large pot of salted water to a boil over high heat. Add the linguine and cook according to the package directions until al dente. Drain and transfer to a large bowl. Toss with 2 tablespoons of the olive oil (to prevent sticking) and set aside.

2. In a large saucepan over medium heat, melt the butter and remaining 2 tablespoons olive oil. Add the garlic, nori powder, salt, red pepper flakes, oregano, sugar, and MSG; stir; and cook until the spices are fragrant and the garlic is golden and aromatic, about 2 minutes.

3. Add the mushrooms and tomato paste to the pan and stir until well combined. Turn the heat to low, cover the pan, and cook for 3 minutes. Add the cherry tomatoes, turn the heat to medium-high, and cook the sauce, stirring often, until the skins of some of the tomatoes begin to loosen, about 5 minutes. Using the back of a spoon, mash half of the tomatoes.

4. Add the vermouth and the vegetable broth to the pan, turn the heat to medium, cover the pan, and cook, stirring occasionally, until the sauce is thin and light with some broken-down tomatoes, 3 to 5 minutes. Uncover the pan and stir in the pepper and lemon zest and juice. Remove the sauce from the heat.

5. Toss the linguine in the sauce and serve immediately.

In the colder months, I rely heavily on ramen to get me through busy days. And since I don't cook with meat or animal fat, I depend on a variety of vegetables, seasonings, and broth for flavor. This ramen recipe is a good example. It includes yuba, which is dried tofu skin, one of my favorite ingredients that lends itself well to ramen. You can find yuba at Asian markets. To kick it up a notch, I top the ramen with chili crisp for added heat.

RAMEN WITH SEARED MAITAKE MUSHROOMS, BOK CHOY & SILKEN TOFU

MAKES 2 SERVINGS

3 tablespoons olive oil

2 green onions, white parts julienned, or thinly sliced, and green parts finely chopped

4 garlic cloves, minced

3 cups vegetable broth

One 4-inch sheet nori, cut into strips with scissors

1 tablespoon white miso paste

1 tablespoon mirin

1 tablespoon soy sauce

1 teaspoon red pepper flakes, plus more for garnishing

1¼ teaspoons kosher salt

½ teaspoon black pepper

Two 3-ounce packets ramen, noodles only

2 medium maitake mushroom steaks (see Cook's Note)

4 heads baby bok choy

2½ ounces yuba, sliced

8 ounces silken tofu, cubed

Crispy onions, black sesame seeds, chili crisp (such as Momofuku Chili Crunch) for garnishing

1. In a small nonstick skillet over medium heat, warm 1 tablespoon of the olive oil until it shimmers. Add the julienned green onions and the garlic and sauté until golden and aromatic, 1 to 2 minutes. Transfer to a medium pot.

2. Set the pot over medium-high heat; add the vegetable broth, half of the nori strips, miso paste, mirin, 1½ teaspoons of the soy sauce, red pepper flakes, 1 teaspoon of the salt, and black pepper; and bring to a boil. Add the ramen, using tongs or chopsticks to break it up as it cooks. Add the maitake mushrooms, bok choy, and yuba, making sure to immerse them fully in the broth for even cooking. After 1 minute, remove the bok choy and mushrooms and set aside on a plate. When the ramen is cooked through, about 3 minutes more, remove the pot from the heat.

3. In a small cast-iron skillet over medium heat, warm the remaining 2 tablespoons olive oil until it shimmers. Add the mushroom steaks and baste with the remaining 1½ teaspoons soy sauce. Using a spatula, press the mushrooms into the pan while they cook to get a good hard sear, about 2 minutes per side. Sprinkle with the remaining ¼ teaspoon salt, remove from the heat, and set aside.

4. Divide the ramen and broth between two bowls and arrange the maitake mushrooms, silken tofu, and bok choy atop the noodles. Garnish with the chopped green onions, crispy onions, remaining nori strips, red pepper flakes, sesame seeds, and chili crisp before serving.

COOK'S NOTE

To create a mushroom "steak," slice the mushrooms into large 4-ounce pieces, about 2 inches thick, cutting through the stem to keep intact as one whole structure.

STICKY SESAME MAITAKE "WINGS"

These maitake "wings" are crispy, sweet, and full of umami flavor. The mushrooms are battered in a coating of flour and cornstarch, fried extra-crispy on the outside and soft on the inside, and then drowned in teriyaki sauce. Maitake mushrooms, also called hen of the woods, have a chicken-like flavor, which you can certainly taste in this dish. Because maitakes have a firm and fleshy consistency, it is easy to cut and shape them without losing their structure. This allows for the creation of distinct chicken wing–like sections when carving, making them a great wing substitute.

MAKES 4 SERVINGS

Special equipment: Deep-fry/candy thermometer

1 cup teriyaki sauce

1 cup chickpea flour

3 tablespoons cornstarch

2 teaspoons poultry seasoning or your favorite all-purpose seasoning blend

½ teaspoon kosher salt

½ teaspoon black pepper

½ cup plant-based milk (such as Oatly) or dairy milk

1 shallot, minced

12 ounces maitake mushroom, cut into "wings" (see Cook's Note)

Neutral oil (such as canola oil or avocado oil) for frying

Chives or thinly sliced green onions and sesame seeds for garnishing

1. Line a baking sheet with parchment paper. Pour the teriyaki sauce into a large bowl and set aside.

2. In a medium bowl, combine the chickpea flour, cornstarch, poultry seasoning, salt, and pepper and stir to mix. Add the milk and shallots, whisking to combine into a batter that is thick, yet pourable.

3. In a medium heavy-bottom pot over medium-high heat, warm 3 inches of neutral oil until it registers 350°F on a deep-fry/candy thermometer.

4. Meanwhile, dip the mushrooms in the batter, one at a time, making sure they're completely covered. Set aside on the prepared baking sheet.

5. When the oil is ready, add the mushrooms in batches and fry, turning them to encourage even cooking, until golden and crispy, about 2 minutes. Drain the mushrooms on paper towels and then toss them with the teriyaki sauce.

6. Serve the "wings" immediately, while crispy and hot, garnished with chives and sesame seeds.

COOK'S NOTE

To make the maitake mushroom "wings," gently pull apart the layers or use a knife to carefully separate the caps along their natural divisions, simply slicing from cap cluster to stem to ensure that the "wing" stays intact through dredging and frying. I like to cut them about the size of a chicken drumstick, or sometimes a little larger.

04

WINTER IS HERE

We meet again, winter—but this time, it appears you've changed. This season feels different, with gentler temperatures, sporadic icy days, and scant snowfall—a curious blend for the East Coast, courtesy of climate change, I reckon. My childhood winters boasted abundant snow, perfect for leaping off our low deck into soft blankets of white. Those towering snowbanks dwarfed me. I'm only five feet tall, after all. Back then, I'd eagerly rise early on school days, awaiting news of impending snowstorms. Snow in the forecast meant no school, snug moments with Mom, and morning cocoa.

This year, no snow muffles the noises of the forest—my footsteps sound loud. Off-season birdsongs perplex me—why do I hear robins? Hints of spring emerge through the frosty earth, like the premature appearance of garlic mustard shoots. The earth is changing and shifting; I sense it. I'm intrigued by the sporadic, unnaturally warm days that allow safe ventures through the woods without icy slips or muddy tumbles. And yet, nostalgia creeps in for the cold months of my childhood.

Winter nudges us to slow down, recharge, and reflect on the year. Festivities grant cherished time with my family, which seems hard to come by these days. Holidays weren't a fixture in my youth; my parents celebrated each day as a gift. As an adult, I have a new appreciation for the depth of their wisdom. Every day is an opportunity for renewal, embracing life's simple pleasures, and pursuing joy.

Foraging gives me something to look forward to during the long cold months. Winter means drinking pine tea and looking for hickory trees to collect bark and make syrup. Without an abundance of snow, I can easily spy the bright red winterberries covering the ground. Rose hips sweeten on the beachfront, ready to be used for tonic. But my all-time favorite part of winter is its transition to spring, which is maple-syrup season. Collecting maple syrup is a labor of love. It teaches patience and appreciation for where the food we enjoy comes from and the effort that goes into producing it. Most of all, it teaches us to be grateful for nature and all that it provides. After a day of boiling sap into syrup, nothing is sweeter than a homemade batch you can store and relish the rest of the year, when the trees are no longer producing. It's beautiful.

Once, I rebuffed winter's embrace, detesting the cold despite my love of the snow. Brian, my late friend, illuminated the value in every season, fostering love for nature's diverse facets. I now understand that, just like plants, humans too need winter's reprieve.

The shagbark hickory tree is one of my favorite trees from which to forage. It has a shaggy, scruffy bark reminiscent of something from a Dr. Seuss book. After you have identified the tree the first time, you'll never miss another. Hickory trees produce delicious nuts. Their aromatic bark can be used for a variety of culinary purposes, including smoking meats, fish, and veggies and making syrups. It's important that when harvesting hickory bark, you only remove pieces from the outer layer that give easily. The shaggier and more separated the bark pieces are from the tree trunk, the better they are for harvesting. If you harvest too much bark from one tree, you may end up hurting it, so always be mindful of sustainable harvesting practices. There are several species of shagbark hickory growing in the Northeast. Although the bark can be harvested year-round, I like to save it for a winter treat. Nuts can be collected from the ground shortly after they have fallen. Examine them for small holes before collecting, as they are often eaten by little weevils.

SHAGBARK HICKORY
(CARYA OVATA)

Appearance: Tree bark first appears smooth and gray when young, transforming into shaggy, grayish brown vertical strips separating from the trunk of the tree. Leaves grow 8 to 16 inches long and alternately arranged on twigs, with 5 to 7 leaflets producing fine-toothed margins. Round nuts, each encased in a hard, four-ribbed shell, itself encased in a thick husk, which changes from green to brown as it ripens. Full-grown trees typically 70 to 80 feet tall, sometimes growing up to 100 feet.

Smell: Bark smells indistinct, but slightly sweet. Becomes pungent with sweet and savory notes once heat is applied.

Taste: Nuts have a texture similar to walnuts and are minty and sweet. Bark is smoky, buttery, rich, and nutty in flavor once heated.

Habitat: Open forest and woodlands alongside oaks, maples, beeches, and more. Prefers deep, well-drained soils rich in organic matter. Often found near streams and rivers.

Region: Throughout most of eastern United States and Canada. From Georgia, Alabama, Mississippi, Louisiana, and some parts of eastern Texas through southeastern Nebraska and Minnesota, and northward to southern Ontario and southern Quebec.

Growth Cycle: Annual, with seeds present from late summer into fall.

Prime Harvest Season: Bark can be harvested year-round. Nuts ripen and begin to fall from trees in late summer and early fall.

Dangerous Lookalikes: None.

HICKORY BOURBON TART WITH CHOCOLATE GANACHE

I am very much a dessert person. Most people who cook do not bake, and vice versa, but I love to do both! This hickory bourbon tart is rich and decadent in the best ways. Shagbark hickory nuts are similar to pecans and walnuts, but nuttier and more delicious. They have a deep, buttery flavor that is slightly sweet, with no bitterness, making them a perfect ingredient for pies and tarts. The natural sweetness of the bourbon complements the slightly sweet taste of the nuts and adds complexity. The chocolate ganache is creamy, and it all comes together to create the perfect dessert.

MAKES 8 TO 10 SERVINGS

Special equipment: 8- or 9-inch tart pan with a removable bottom

Tart Shell

1¾ cups all-purpose flour, or as needed

⅔ cup confectioners' sugar

½ teaspoon vanilla powder (see Cook's Note, page 50), or 1 teaspoon vanilla extract

¼ teaspoon kosher salt

½ cup salted, plant-based butter (such as Country Crock avocado oil) or dairy butter, cold and cubed

2 tablespoons ice water

1 tablespoon neutral oil (such as canola oil or avocado oil)

Filling

1½ cups shagbark hickory nuts, coarsely chopped

⅔ cup dark brown sugar

½ cup salted, plant-based butter (such as Country Crock avocado oil) or dairy butter, cubed

3 tablespoons golden syrup (such as Lyle's)

3 tablespoons plant-based heavy whipping cream (such as Silk) or dairy heavy whipping cream

2 tablespoons bourbon

Juice of ½ lemon

½ teaspoon vanilla extract

continued

1. Preheat the oven to 350°F.

2. To make the tart shell: In a food processor, combine the flour, confectioners' sugar, vanilla powder (if using), and salt. Pulse until the ingredients are just combined, about 5 seconds. Add the butter and pulse until the mixture is coarse and crumbly, about 1 minute.

3. In a small liquid measuring cup, combine the ice water and neutral oil (and vanilla extract, if using) and mix with a fork. Slowly stream the water-oil mixture into the food processor while it's running, and run until the ingredients come together in a smooth, loose ball of dough, about 1 minute. If it's too sticky, add another 1 tablespoon flour. (Alternatively, if you don't have a food processor, in a large bowl, whisk the dry ingredients together and use your fingers to work in the butter. Using a rubber spatula, incorporate the water-oil mixture into the dough and then use your hands to form a ball.)

4. Press the dough evenly into an 8- or 9-inch tart pan with a removable bottom, beginning in the center and moving toward and up the edge of the pan. If needed, use the bottom of a drinking glass to help smooth out the tart shell. Trim the excess dough from the edges and smooth the edges with your finger. Using a fork, pierce the bottom of the tart shell several times.

5. Bake the shell until pale gold, 25 to 30 minutes. Remove from the oven, but do not turn the oven off.

6. To make the filling: Meanwhile, place the chopped hickory nuts on a baking sheet and toast alongside the tart shell for 5 minutes. Remove from the oven and set aside.

7. In a medium saucepan over medium-high heat, combine the brown sugar, butter, golden syrup, heavy cream, bourbon, lemon juice, and vanilla extract and stir to combine. When the butter begins to melt, add the toasted nuts and bring to a boil, stirring constantly, about 5 minutes. Remove from the heat and set aside.

HICKORY BOURBON TART WITH
CHOCOLATE GANACHE CONTINUED

Ganache

¼ cup chopped semisweet chocolate

¼ cup your favorite plant-based heavy whipping cream (such as Silk) or dairy heavy whipping cream

Flaky sea salt for garnish (optional)

Vanilla ice cream for serving

8. Pour the filling evenly into the tart shell, using a rubber spatula to spread it out. Return the tart to the oven, and bake until the center is bubbly and the edges are a deep golden brown, 20 to 30 minutes. Place on a wire rack and let cool for 30 minutes.

9. To make the ganache: Put the chocolate in a small bowl and set aside.

10. In a small saucepan over medium-high heat, bring the heavy cream to a simmer. Once small bubbles form, remove from the heat and pour the hot cream over the chocolate. Using a rubber spatula, stir until smooth and creamy.

11. Using the rubber spatula, evenly spread the chocolate ganache over the filling. Refrigerate the tart so the ganache sets and hardens, at least 30 minutes or up to 1 hour. (Or freeze, well wrapped, for up to 2 months.)

12. When ready to serve, bring the tart to room temperature, then remove from the pan by gently pushing up from the bottom to release from the ring. If you like, gently slide the bottom from underneath the tart and place the tart on a tray or serving plate. Sprinkle the tart with flaky sea salt (if using), top each slice with a scoop of ice cream, and enjoy.

The easiest way to permeate a dish or drink with the smoky, sweet, and nutty flavors of shagbark hickory is to use this simple syrup. It works as a base for many recipes, including cocktails and desserts, and is great in coffee. The possibilities are endless, and once you taste shagbark hickory syrup, you may even consider using it for pancakes instead of maple syrup. Its flavor is unique and rich, almost creamy on the palate. This recipe doesn't require much, just a bit of time and patience. For the best-tasting syrup, you'll want to pick bark pieces that are clean of any lichens, which are pale-green, bitter-tasting organisms that grow on trees and rocks. This syrup requires equal parts sugar and water to be shelf-stable, so be sure to measure your shagbark hickory tea after it is fully infused to calculate the exact amount of sugar you will need.

SHAGBARK HICKORY SYRUP

1. Preheat the oven to 350°F.

2. Wash the hickory bark under cold running water, pat dry, and then place on a baking sheet. Bake the bark until it smells smoky and sweet, about 25 minutes.

3. In a large pot over medium-high heat, combine the bark and enough water to cover completely and bring to a boil. Turn the heat to low and let simmer until this tea is dark amber in color, about 30 minutes.

4. Discard the bark and strain the tea into a liquid measuring cup, and then pour it into another large pot, to determine the volume. Measure out an equal volume of the sugar.

5. Add the sugar to the tea, set over medium heat, and let simmer until the tea has reduced by about half and is quite thick and syrupy, 45 minutes to 1 hour.

6. Pour the finished syrup into the sterilized mason jar, leaving ½ inch of head space, and seal tightly.

7. The syrup will keep for up to 3 months in the refrigerator, or up to 1 year in the freezer.

MAKES ABOUT 4 CUPS

Special equipment: One 32-ounce sterilized mason jar (see page 15)

1 pound shagbark hickory bark, broken into small pieces

4 cups water, or as needed

4 cups pure cane sugar, or as needed

This is my favorite dairy-free ice cream. The base is coconut, which gives it a creamy texture. But the most pronounced flavors are the shagbark hickory syrup, ground coffee, and grated chocolate that are mixed in, and the taste of infused hickory smoke is mind-blowing. I got to share this recipe during my television debut on the PBS show *A Moveable Feast*. Many nonvegans loved the delicacy and couldn't believe it was dairy-free. Those moments are always rewarding. I was inspired to create this recipe after trying a hazelnut–espresso bean ice cream from Arethusa Farm when I was a vegetarian. This is my re-creation, but with a dairy-free twist.

SHAGBARK HICKORY ICE CREAM

1. In the blender, combine the coconut cream, condensed milk, ground espresso beans, hickory syrup, vanilla, and salt and blend until smooth, 1 to 2 minutes.

2. Pour the mixture into the frozen bowl of the ice-cream maker. Stir in the chocolate and then churn until mostly frozen and creamy, about 25 minutes. (Alternatively, if you don't have an ice-cream maker, pour the mixture into the loaf pan, and stir in the chocolate. Press a sheet of plastic wrap on the surface of the mixture, making sure it's completely covered to avoid crystallization during the freezing process. Freeze for 4 hours.)

3. Scoop the ice cream into individual bowls, garnish each serving with an edible flower, and savor every bite. You won't be disappointed!

MAKES 4 TO 6 SERVINGS

Special equipment: High-speed blender, ice-cream maker (optional), 9 by 5-inch metal loaf pan

One 13.5-ounce can heavy coconut cream, chilled overnight in the refrigerator or for 2 hours in the freezer

1½ cups sweetened condensed oat or coconut milk (such as Nature's Charm)

¼ cup coarsely ground espresso beans

3 tablespoons Shagbark Hickory Syrup (page 223)

1 teaspoon vanilla extract, or 1 vanilla bean, split and scraped

1 pinch kosher salt

¼ cup grated or roughly chopped dark chocolate

Edible flowers (such as calendula or micro nasturtium) for garnishing

Explore the versatile applications of shagbark hickory with this savory leek recipe. While typically associated with sweet syrup, shagbark hickory also excels as a smoking agent to infuse delightful smoky notes into your favorite vegetables and proteins. Embracing the cozy allure of winter, this dish offers a comforting warmth, allowing the flavors of seasonal vegetables to shine. The cauliflower cream perfectly complements the earthy taste of charred leeks, making it a great winter appetizer.

SMOKED LEEKS WITH CAULIFLOWER CREAM

1. In a large bowl, combine the shagbark hickory and enough water to cover and let soak for 30 minutes.

2. Prepare the grill for medium-high heat (or preheat the oven to 425°F).

3. To make the cauliflower cream: In a blender, combine the cauliflower, vegetable broth, milk, butter, garlic, and half the lemon juice and pulse to a smooth consistency, similar to crème fraîche. Transfer to a medium bowl and set aside.

4. In a small bowl, combine the remaining lemon juice, the neutral oil, smoked paprika, coriander, cumin, sugar, salt, and a few cranks of black pepper and mix well.

5. Place the leeks on a baking sheet and, using a basting brush, coat them with the lemon-oil mixture, saving the rest for basting while cooking.

6. Remove the bark from the water. Place the bark and leeks on the grill (or put the bark and leeks on the baking sheet if using the oven).

7. Grill the leeks until tender, fragrant, and charred all over, 15 to 20 minutes; basting at the 7-minute mark, and turning the leeks every few minutes for even charring. (Or bake for 35 to 40 minutes, basting every 10 to 15 minutes, until no more marinade remains.)

8. Using a spoon, smear a generous amount of cauliflower cream on the bottom of a serving plate. Top with the leeks, and garnish with a dash of smoked paprika. Enjoy hot.

MAKES 4 SERVINGS

1 large piece shagbark hickory bark

Cauliflower Cream

2 cups cauliflower florets

¼ cup vegetable broth

2 tablespoons plant-based milk (such as Oatly) or dairy milk

1 tablespoon plant-based butter (such as Country Crock avocado oil) or dairy butter

2 garlic cloves

Juice of 1 lemon

2 tablespoons neutral oil (such as canola oil or avocado oil)

1 teaspoon smoked paprika, plus more for garnishing

½ teaspoon ground coriander

½ teaspoon ground cumin

½ teaspoon pure cane sugar

½ teaspoon kosher salt

Black pepper

2 large leeks, halved lengthwise

PINE
(PINUS)

There are approximately thirty-five species of pine trees native to the United States and, including non-native trees, approximately fifty-seven species throughout North America. Pines are considered conifers, meaning plants that have cones and leaves resembling needles or scales. Most pines are typically woody trees. Some have the traditional Christmas-tree form, with triangular crowns, but most pines have a broader base and less-steep sides. Pines can look like large overgrown shrubs or the tall trees recognizable to most people. They can be hard pines, which have two or three needles per bundle, or soft pines, which have five needles per bundle. Pine trees can be identified by their aromatic scent, particularly the pinyon pine, which produces pine nuts and is found in the desert habitats of the American Southwest. Pines are magnificent trees that can live for more than four hundred years and grow in a variety of environments. Most parts of the *Pinus* species are edible, including the cones, seeds, needles, and pollen. In this section, we'll examine three species: the eastern white pine, the pinyon pine, and the sugar pine.

Appearance: Best identified by their cones and needles, which are often arranged in fascicles—bundles of needles growing together in clusters of two, three, or five on the branches. Each species has varying cone shapes and sizes, as well as needle lengths. Most *Pinus* species have very straight trunks.

Eastern white pine Grows to 80 feet or more. Needles are blue-green, fluffy, slender, and arranged in bundles of five in clusters along the branches. Trunk is straight with horizontal branches that form a conical or pyramidal shape. Bark of young trees is smooth and silver-gray in color. Becomes dark, thick, and scaly, with deep furrows and ridges, with age. Produces cylindrical cones that are long and slender, measuring 4 to 8 inches in length.

Pinyon pine Grows to 40 feet or more. Needles are dark green, short, stout, ridged, often twisted, typically 1 to 2 inches in length, and are arranged in bundles of two. Trunk is short and stout, with a slightly irregular shape. Branches are short and spreading, giving way to a rounded or irregular crown. Distinct branching pattern, with lower branches appearing on the trunk in a layered fashion. Branches are densely arranged. Bark is deeply furrowed, rough, and thick, typically forming an intricate pattern, and ranging from gray to reddish brown in color.

Sugar pine Grows up to 200 feet. Trunk is thick, with a diameter of 5 to 6 feet. Open irregular crown. Needles are dark green, slightly twisted in appearance, and long and slender, growing between 2 to 4 inches in length and arranged in clusters of five; occasionally three or four. Bark is reddish to brown to grayish brown in color, rough, and thick, developing deep furrows and becoming scaly and pleated with age. Produces both male and female cones. Male cones produce pollen in spring and are small and cylindrical, usually appearing yellow or reddish brown. Female cones are significantly larger, 10 to 20 inches in length, and have scales with sharp, curved tips.

Smell

Eastern white pine Sweet, fresh, acidic, refreshing, crisp.

Pinyon pine Distinct, pleasant aromatic scent from resin produced on trunk. On warm, sunny days, they smell slightly nutty due to the seeds.

Sugar pine Strong pleasant, yet resinous scent. Hints of vanilla or butterscotch.

Taste

Eastern white pine Needles are herbal, sweet, aromatic; reminiscent of perfume.

Pinyon pine Needles are resinous, mildly citrusy, and subtly sweet. Seeds are buttery, nutty, creamy, and subtly piney in flavor.

Sugar pine Needles are resinous and mildly citrusy, sometimes bitter and slightly astringent. Seeds are sweet, resinous, and buttery in flavor, and often described as sweeter compared to other pine nut varieties.

Habitat

Eastern white pine Often found in mixed forests, and sandy or rocky soils. Prefers well-drained sites; tolerant of various environmental conditions.

Pinyon pine Prefers rocky, sandy, or gravelly soils. Very drought tolerant.

Sugar pine Often grows in mountainous regions, particularly mixed conifer forests. Thrives in regions with moderate to heavy snowfall.

Eastern white pine Often found throughout New England, New York, Pennsylvania, New Jersey, the Great Lakes, the upper Midwest, and across Canada.

Pinyon pine Native to the southwestern United States and grows throughout Arizona, New Mexico, Utah, Colorado, Nevada, and parts of southeastern California.

Sugar pine Primarily found in the western United States from Oregon and California, down to Baja California in Mexico.

Growth Cycle: Evergreen, meaning they retain their needles and green color throughout the year and do not undergo the same leaf-shedding cycle as deciduous trees. This enables them to photosynthesize and produce energy even during the colder months. Seeds are located in cones, and most species have winged seeds that are dispersed by wind, while others have seeds that are dispersed by birds.

Prime Harvest Season: Cones are best harvested when young, in summer months. Needles can be harvested all year long.

Dangerous Lookalikes: Yew pine. Toxic to humans and identifiable by their flat, short, dark green needles. Back of each needle is lighter green and has no stripes running length of needle, which makes it easier to identify. Not native to North America, but grow in southeastern parts of the United States in Florida, Georgia, Alabama, and Mississippi.

As a kid, I loved ginger ale and Sprite. They were the cure-alls in our Jamaican household. Stomachache? Ginger ale or Sprite, every time! This soda was inspired by food bloggers Ms. Shi and Mr. He, who make a drink with pine needles that's similar to Sprite. As soon as I tasted it, I knew I had to try to make my own, while keeping it as close to the real deal as possible! This flavorful duplicate isn't overpowered by the pine; it's a refreshing, natural soda. Keep in mind, it will take 3 days of fermentation before you are able to enjoy this sweet, bubbly drink!

PINE SODA

MAKES 4 SERVINGS

Special equipment: Sterilized 16-ounce mason jar (see page 15)

2 cups pine needles, woody ends removed

⅓ cup pure cane sugar

2 cups filtered water

Ice cubes

Juice of 1 lemon

Juice of 1 lime

4 lemon or lime wedges

1. In a colander, rinse the pine needles under cold running water to remove excess dirt and debris, 10 to 15 seconds. Pat the needles dry with paper towels and set aside until they are almost completely dry, so the natural yeast that develops during fermentation can do its work. Transfer to the sterilized mason jar.

2. Add the sugar and filtered water to the jar, screw on the lid, and shake the mixture vigorously until the sugar dissolves. Remove the lid and place a fresh sheet of paper towel over the mason jar, then secure with the ring from the mason jar lid.

3. Place the jar in front of a sunny window for 6 to 8 hours. (This will speed up the fermentation process.) Remove the paper towel and seal the mason jar with the original lid. Shake once more and return to the sunny window for 3 days. Do not shake the bottle any further during this time.

4. On Day 3, you will notice carbon dioxide bubbles in the drink. This means that the soda has fermented properly and is ready to be consumed.

5. Fill four glasses with ice. Unscrew the lid of the mason jar and stir in the lemon juice and lime juice. Pour the soda into the glasses, and garnish with the lemon or lime wedges. Enjoy the same day, as this soda won't keep!

These shortbread cookies are herbaceous and jam-packed with flavor, making them a winter staple. They're sweet, crumbly, and buttery, but also savory from the peppercorn and pine. The result is a perfectly balanced cookie. I prefer them without icing, but you can enjoy with a simple icing made of lemon, your favorite milk, and confectioners' sugar. These are the adult shortbread cookies you've been waiting for!

PINK PEPPERCORN– PINE SHORTBREAD COOKIES

1. Preheat the oven to 375°F. Line a baking sheet with parchment paper. Set aside.

2. In a medium bowl, combine the flour, pine needles, peppercorns, and salt and whisk to incorporate.

3. In the bowl of a stand mixer, combine the butter, confectioners' sugar, and vanilla and cream on low speed until smooth. (Alternatively, in a large bowl, using a large spoon or spatula, combine the butter and vanilla and mash until smooth, then stir in the confectioners' sugar.)

4. With the mixer still on low speed, add the flour mixture and mix well, scraping down the sides of the bowl as needed, 3 to 4 minutes. Slowly stream in the ice water, a little at a time, until you have a soft, tacky, and cohesive dough. (If you're not using a mixer, stir with a rubber spatula until the ingredients are combined, then add the ice water, a little at a time, mixing with your hands, until the dough is cohesive.)

5. On a lightly floured work surface, form the dough into a 4 by 5-inch rectangle. Wrap in plastic wrap and refrigerate until firm, 30 minutes to 1 hour.

6. Roll out the dough into a ⅓- to ½-inch-thick, 8-inch square. Cut it into small circles or rectangles or use a cookie cutter to cut into your favorite shape.

7. Place the cookies on the prepared baking sheet, and sprinkle evenly with the vanilla sugar. If you like, you can gently press a pine needle into the center of each cookie.

8. Bake the cookies for 12 to 15 minutes, rotating the baking sheet halfway through. Let cool before serving.

MAKES 14 TO 16 COOKIES

Special equipment: Stand mixer (optional)

1½ cups all-purpose flour, plus more for the work surface

¼ cup pine needles, minced, plus more for garnishing (optional)

2 teaspoons coarsely ground pink peppercorns

½ teaspoon kosher salt

½ cup plant-based butter (such as Country Crock avocado oil) or dairy butter, at room temperature and cut into pieces

⅓ cup confectioners' sugar

½ teaspoon vanilla extract

1 to 2 tablespoons ice water

2 tablespoons vanilla sugar

CAFÉ BRÛLOT

You can find café brûlot on the streets of New Orleans. *Brûlot* means "burnt brandy" in French. I was introduced to this coffee drink by a friend's stepmother, who was raving about it when she returned from a trip to New Orleans. I wrote down the bare bones of her description and made my own at home. It did not disappoint. It's a richly aromatic coffee, enlivened by spices and fresh orange. This is a flamed drink, so proceed with caution. If you don't drink coffee, you can prepare this with your favorite coffee alternative, and it will be equally delicious. Since the alcohol is cooked off during the flaming process, leaving a myriad of deep flavors, you can enjoy this beverage even if you don't drink. For a Jamaican twist, I like to add a few sorrel flowers as a special treat. Mix and match your own favorite spices and omit any aromatics that you don't want, but keep the orange peel, cloves, coffee, and brandy for the sake of authenticity.

MAKES 4 SERVINGS

Special equipment: Brûlot bowl or a deep heavy-bottom pot, long-handled ladle, long matches

6 whole cloves

1 orange, peeled in a spiral still attached to the flesh

Peel of 1 lemon, cut into strips

1 handful fresh pine needles

½-inch piece fresh ginger

3 allspice berries

2 cardamom pods

1 vanilla bean, halved

1 cinnamon stick

¼ teaspoon ground nutmeg

1 ounce Grand Marnier or triple sec

2 ounces VSOP cognac (such as Martell) or bourbon

3 tablespoons brown sugar

3 cups freshly brewed coffee or coffee alternative (such as Postum)

Citrus peel for garnishing

1. Press a clove into the spiralized orange peel every 1 to 2 inches. Pierce the orange with a fork to act as a handle.

2. Place the brûlot bowl or a deep, heavy-bottom pot over medium heat. Add the lemon peel, pine needles, ginger, allspice berries, cardamom pods, vanilla bean, cinnamon stick, and nutmeg, and, using the back of a ladle, lightly crush the spices to release their aromatics, about 1 minute.

3. Remove the brûlot bowl from the heat and add the Grand Marnier and cognac. Using a long match or a long lighter, carefully ignite the liqueur; it will appear bright blue. Using the fork, hold the orange above the bowl. Using the ladle, pour the flaming liquid over the orange. Repeat until the flames disappear.

4. Using a sieve, remove and discard the lemon peel, pine needles, ginger, allspice, cardamom, vanilla, cinnamon, and nutmeg. Add the brown sugar and coffee and stir well to combine.

5. Ladle the café brûlot into cups, garnish with citrus peel, and enjoy while it's hot.

MAPLE
(ACER SACCHARUM)

I must admit, few things in nature offer as much joy and abundance as a maple tree. The sweet sap flows freely from the trunks and, when boiled down, it provides rich, sweet goodness with a range of flavor profiles. Maple trees have a rich history. Indigenous people from the woodlands of Canada to the northeastern United States have been relying on and utilizing maple trees for thousands of years. There are several maple species, including black, red, sugar, and silver maples, which can all be tapped for their sap. In this section, I cover only black, red, and sugar maples, as silver maple sap is often bitter and off-putting. Black maples have a strong, robust, and full-bodied taste with hints of caramel and molasses. Red maples are lighter and slightly sweeter, with vanilla or floral undertones, but can sometimes exhibit some bitterness or off-flavors depending on their age and habitat. Sugar maples are the most special. They have the highest sugar content and a balanced, delicate flavor that is smooth and buttery with hints of caramel and vanilla. Due to their high sugar content, they are typically preferred for tapping as it makes the process of boiling sap easier and yields the tastiest syrup.

Maple trees are the first to wake up, from late winter to early spring. In early February, maple syrup tends to be light and delicate in flavor and color. As spring approaches, the flavor and color changes, becoming deeper and richer. The process of making syrup is long and time-consuming. The trees produce a clear, thin sap, which is boiled down for hours before becoming what we know as "maple syrup." A whopping forty gallons of sap is needed to produce one gallon of syrup! The best and easiest time to identify maple trees is in early spring, when they flower, and late spring and summer, before they drop their leaves.

Appearance

Black maple Three-lobed leaves, thick, with a few coarse teeth along leaf margins and hairy undersides. Dark green on the upper surface and yellowish green beneath, turning yellow or brownish yellow, sometimes tinged with red, during foliage season. Bark is more furrowed and darker than sugar maple bark. Clusters of small yellow flowers and winged fruit appear in early spring.

Red maple Reddish, three-lobed leaves while in foliage, with serrated margins and pointed tips. Smooth, light-gray bark when young; dark gray and rough when mature, often with peeling flakes present. Lower branches sweep upward. Fruit winged seeds with long, drooping stems, usually red to green at first, and tan when mature. Often confused with sugar

maple due to bark similarities when young. Main difference when young are dense, red flower clusters appearing on red maples in March or April.

Sugar maple Five-lobed leaves with a few large teeth. Leaves are yellow to crimson during fall foliage season and otherwise bright green at the top and paler green below. Trees have symmetrical crowns. Twigs are smooth and reddish brown; bark is grayish brown and smooth when young; fissured with large, long irregular flakes when mature. Long stalks of yellowish-green flower clusters appear in early spring.

Smell: Indistinct.

Taste: Sap of the sugar maple is sweetest.

Habitat

Black maple Thrives in dense shade and needs a large area for growth. Commonly grow in moist soils of river bottoms in mixed hardwood forests.

Red maple Thrives in bright sun and partial shade. Urban tolerant and are often planted in city parks. Do best in moist areas, but grow in diverse sites, from dry ridges to peat bogs and swamps.

Sugar maple Thrives in shady woodland areas as well as partial-sun environments. Urban intolerant and grow on sand, sandy loams, and well-drained soils. Does not grow well in dry, shallow soil.

Region

Black maple Grows in central and eastern regions of North America. Can be found in parts of eastern United States, including Missouri, Illinois, Indiana, Ohio, Kentucky, Tennessee, and West Virginia. Also found in southern Ontario and southwestern Quebec in Canada.

Red maple Widely scattered across North America in eastern and central regions. Found in abundance along East Coast, including Maine, New Hampshire, Massachusetts, New York, Connecticut, Pennsylvania, and as far south as Florida and Texas. Also present in Midwest and Great Lakes region, including Michigan, Wisconsin, and Illinois. Can be found from southern Canada, including parts of Ontario and Quebec, all the way up to Newfoundland and Labrador in the north.

Sugar maple Primarily found in eastern part of North America. Can be found from northern parts of Georgia and Alabama, extending northward into New England and Great Lakes region. Particular abundance in states such as Vermont, New Hampshire, New York, and Pennsylvania. In Canada, widespread in Ontario and Quebec, as well as parts of New Brunswick and Nova Scotia.

Growth Cycle: Deciduous, meaning they shed their leaves every winter. In spring, branches bud and leaf out, producing flowers, and then seed pods. Grows and matures in summer. Leaves change colors in fall and drop in winter.

Prime Harvest Season: Sometimes late January, but typically February to April, when temperatures are below freezing at night, and days are warm and bright.

Dangerous Lookalikes: None, however, there are a few maple species that have been noted to have potential toxicity causing skin irritations: boxelder maple and coral bark maple.

Maple syrup season is here! Let's start with the basics. First and foremost, you'll need the right equipment to get the job done. It can seem daunting and expensive, however once you're set up, you'll have the tools needed for a successful maple-syrup season for years to come. Plus, you'll have something fun to do with family and friends every winter. Maple tapping, or sugaring, is one of my favorite group activities, and it's now a tradition in my household. Let's get right into the good stuff, shall we?

EQUIPMENT

You'll need to purchase the proper equipment in order to tap the trees as efficiently as possible. If you have plenty of maple trees, you might want to consider a tubing system, which allows the sap to flow by gravity, utilizing the natural pressure created by changes in temperature and atmospheric conditions. The collected sap is directed toward a main collection point, such as a storage tank or a vacuum-pump system that helps enhance sap flow. From there, the sap can be further processed in the sugarhouse to make maple syrup. Following are the necessities, listed in order of use.

Drill and Hammer. I recommend having a drill and hammer on hand. You'll need to drill into the tree just enough for the sap to flow, and gently hammer the taps into each hole. A $\frac{7}{16}$-inch drill bit is the proper size for tapping.

Taps, Collection Buckets and Lids, and Hooks. A tap allows the tree's sap to drip into a sap collection bucket. The lid will help keep out bird droppings, bugs, and rainwater. You'll also need hooks to keep the tap and bucket lid connected to the bucket. Buy stainless-steel or metal equipment, so that you can use it for years to come. Tractor Supply has a wonderful metal-bucket starter kit that comes with everything you'll need!

Storage Buckets. To amass the syrup from the collection buckets that are attached to the trees, you'll need large storage buckets. These are necessary so that after emptying the collection buckets, you can return them to the trees to collect more sap. Five- to ten-gallon food-grade buckets with lids are perfect for this. You can easily find them at your local hardware store or online.

Large Shallow Pan or Evaporator. For boiling the sap over a heat source, such as a propane burner or a wood fire.

Outdoor Burners with Gas Hookup and Propane Tanks. The best place to boil the sap is outdoors. When you boil sap in the kitchen, sugary residue evaporates and gets stuck to all the

surfaces and ceiling. I live in a log cabin, and the first time I did this, things got ugly. By the end of the day, everything was sticky, and the amount of steam produced during evaporation could peel off wallpaper. So it's simply not worth it. I recommend using an outdoor two-burner gas cooktop.

Finishing Pot. For the final product, you'll need a smaller finishing pot. I suggest a 3- to 4-quart finishing pot for when the maple syrup is getting very close to boiling temperature and is ready to be strained and stored. As previously stated, it takes forty gallons of maple sap to make one gallon of maple syrup. If you're making maple syrup at home with a simple setup, you likely won't be making close to that. A 3.7-quart finishing pot has always been ideal for me, and I have an entire maple grove on the side of my yard. I recommend a pot that has a pour spout, so that you don't accidentally lose any maple when bottling.

Maple Filtration Kit. When your maple syrup has reached the proper temperature and is ready to store, you'll need filters to filter out any sediment. I pour my sap through a large strainer into the boiling pot before cooking it down, to avoid as many impurities in the final product as I can. When you put so much time into making your own maple syrup, you want to see a clear finished product, without sand or other particles. This way, you can enjoy every drop. I suggest getting a maple filtration kit, which can be used as you are bottling. Find a set that includes reusable filters, a heavy-duty boiling filter, and pre-filters for sap collection.

Mason Jars. Mason jars are the best containers for storing maple syrup. Make sure to sterilize the jars (see page 15) to avoid any bad bacterial growth.

Canner Kit. The easiest way to sterilize mason jars is with a boiling-water bath, so if you purchase a canner kit, which is basically a large pressure cooker or a big enamelware pot, with a basket attachment of sorts, you'll have all of the tools you need.

Candy Thermometer and (optional) Hydrometer. A candy thermometer is essential for determining when your maple syrup has reached the correct temperature for storing. If you want to go a step further, you can also purchase a hydrometer, which allows you to test the sugar content of your finished product.

MAPLE TAPPING

The techniques that we use for tapping maple trees today were originated by the Indigenous peoples of northeastern North America. Here, you'll learn how to successfully tap your own maple trees to collect sap and produce your very own maple syrup!

1. **Check the Weather Conditions.** The best time to tap maple trees is when the temperature is below freezing at night, and above freezing during the day, since sap flows freely under those conditions. This typically occurs in late winter and early spring (between January and early April, depending on your location). Tapping must be completed before the trees bud to avoid the collection of bitter sap. Warm sunny days are best for collecting sap.

2. **Select the Trees.** Identify healthy maple trees that are at least 10 inches in diameter. The larger, the better, as it will equal a greater yield of sap. Trees that are between 10 to 20 inches in diameter should only have one tap and can produce one to ten gallons of sap per year. Trees that are greater than 20 inches in diameter can have two taps and produce ten to sixty gallons of sap per year. Generally, you have a three- to four-week window to collect maple sap after tapping a tree.

3. **Prepare your Equipment.** Gather the necessary equipment, including taps, collection buckets, and tubing (if using a more advanced system). Clean and sterilize the equipment to avoid bacterial contamination.

4. **Tap the Trees.** Choose a spot on the tree trunk at about chest height and drill a small hole 2 to 3 inches deep at a slight upward angle (about 85 degrees). Ideally, the tap hole should be on the south side of the tree above a large root, or below a large branch for optimal sap flow. Gently nudge a tap into the hole firmly but gently with a hammer, until the fit is snug and secure. You should see minimal signs of sap leakage. Then, clear away the shavings from the hole. Attach a collection bucket to the tap to catch the dripping sap, and cover with the lid. If using tubing, connect it to the tap and direct the sap flow into a storage bucket.

5. **Amass the Sap.** Collect the sap regularly, ideally within 24 hours, to prevent spoilage. If you see any bacterial growth on the sap due to factors such as warmer weather, discard it. Store the sap in a cool place until you are ready for processing. If you happen to have an abundance of sap and live in a climate that is snowy, you can store the sap in large, sanitized buckets in a shady area and

covered with snow as it will help to preserve the sap and avoid bacterial contamination while you boil in batches.

6. **Boil and Evaporate.** Strain the sap through a mesh sieve to remove any impurities. Pour the collected sap into a large, shallow pan or evaporator and set over an outdoor heat source, such as a propane burner or a wood-burning stove. Boil the sap to evaporate the water content and concentrate the sugars. This process can take up to 7 hours, and the sap will gradually darken and start to smell syrupy. Be sure to skim impurities off of the top throughout the cooking process, so that your finished product will be as pure and clear as possible. Once the sap has reduced by at least 50 percent, pour it into a large stockpot over high heat for the final 1 or 2 hours of cooking. Once the sap reduces further by about half, transfer it to the finishing pot.

7. **Finish and Filter.** Once the sap reaches the desired consistency (66 to 67 percent sugar content—you can purchase a hydrometer for this reading), remove it from the heat. Alternatively, when the syrup reaches 7°F above the boiling point of water at your location, test it with a spoon to check for consistency—it should be thick, yet pourable. If it's too thin, watch it carefully and give it another minute to thicken up before removing from the heat. Filter the syrup through a fine mesh or cheesecloth, or follow the directions on your filtration kit, to remove any impurities or sediment.

8. **Store.** Pour the finished syrup into sterilized containers, such as glass jars or bottles, and seal them tightly. Store in a cool, dark place or in the refrigerator to maintain its quality and extend its shelf life. The syrup can last for up to a year at room temperature. Refrigerate after opening. Once opened, it can last for several months.

I ate bacon once in my life. As a lifelong vegetarian, I caved just one time. On my first trip to Canada in April 2016, I tried a small piece of Canadian bacon. I would be lying if I said I wasn't blown away. I was determined to create something crispy, smoky, and sweet to accompany a savory breakfast. This banana peel–maple "bacon" does just that, and more.

BANANA PEEL– MAPLE "BACON"

MAKES 3 OR 4 SERVINGS

3 tablespoons tamari or soy sauce

2 tablespoons maple syrup

1½ teaspoons rice vinegar

1 teaspoon liquid smoke

2 teaspoons light brown sugar

½ teaspoon smoked paprika

½ teaspoon smoked salt

½ teaspoon cracked black pepper

Peels of 3 overripe, almost black, organic bananas, flesh gently scraped off

1 tablespoon neutral oil (such as canola oil or avocado oil)

1. In a medium bowl, combine the tamari, maple syrup, rice vinegar, liquid smoke, brown sugar, smoked paprika, smoked salt, and black pepper and whisk to incorporate. Set this marinade aside.

2. Cut the banana peels lengthwise into two strips each and add to the marinade. Place in the refrigerator and let soak for 30 minutes.

3. In a large skillet over medium-high heat, warm the neutral oil until it shimmers. Add the banana peels and cook until brown and crispy and small bubbles form, 1 to 2 minutes per side.

4. Enjoy the "bacon" immediately; it does not store well.

Brussels sprouts are a wintertime favorite. They're in season during the winter months, which is when their nutritional value and flavor are at their best. To folks who don't love brussels sprouts, I implore you to try this recipe. I promise it will not disappoint. When roasted over high heat, you get crispy, flavorful pieces of the vegetable, especially with the addition of maple syrup. These brussels sprouts are smoky and sweet, and have a nice crunch from toasted pine nuts. If you don't like pine nuts, swap them out for your favorite toasted nut such as almonds or cashews.

MAPLE-ROASTED BRUSSELS SPROUTS

1. Preheat the oven to 425°F. Line a baking sheet with parchment paper.

2. In a medium bowl, combine the maple syrup, avocado oil, balsamic vinegar, garlic, shallot, smoked paprika, onion powder, kosher salt, black pepper, and cayenne and stir to incorporate. Add the brussels sprouts and toss to coat well. Place the brussels sprouts on the prepared baking sheet, spreading them in an even, single layer.

3. Roast the brussels sprouts until crispy and caramelized, 15 to 20 minutes, stirring or shaking the pan every 5 to 10 minutes for even cooking.

4. Transfer the brussels sprouts to a serving platter, garnish with Parmesan cheese and toasted pine nuts, and sprinkle with flaky salt. Enjoy immediately.

MAKES 4 SERVINGS

3 tablespoons maple syrup (see page 239)

2 tablespoons avocado oil

1½ teaspoons balsamic vinegar

4 garlic cloves, minced

1 shallot, minced

½ teaspoon smoked paprika

1 teaspoon onion powder

1 teaspoon kosher salt

½ teaspoon cracked black pepper

¼ teaspoon cayenne pepper

1 pound brussels sprouts, halved

Grated Parmesan cheese and toasted pine nuts (see Cook's Note, page 27) for garnishing

Flaky sea salt

MAPLE-BUTTER CINNAMON ROLLS

I could eat these cinnamon rolls every morning! They're ooey-gooey, soft, and fluffy, making them the perfect winter treat. They're not overly sweet, so the maple butter balances them beautifully. The flaxseed meal and water combination works like eggs and is a great replacement for baking.

MAKES 10 TO 12 ROLLS

Special equipment: Stand mixer with dough hook, 9-inch round cake pan or 9 by 13-inch baking pan

Dough

2 tablespoons flaxseed meal

¼ cup plus 2 tablespoons water

½ cup plant-based milk (such as Oatly) or dairy milk

3 tablespoons plant-based butter (such as Country Crock avocado oil) or dairy butter, melted

2 tablespoons brewed coffee

2¾ cups all-purpose flour, or as needed

⅓ cup pure cane sugar

2¼ teaspoons instant yeast

1 teaspoon kosher salt

1 teaspoon ground cinnamon

¼ teaspoon ground nutmeg

Filling

½ cup packed brown sugar

1 tablespoon ground cinnamon

¼ cup plant-based butter (such as Country Crock avocado oil) or dairy butter, at room temperature

2 tablespoons coconut cream, warmed in the microwave

Maple Butter

1 cup maple syrup

½ cup plant-based butter (such as Country Crock avocado oil) or dairy butter, melted

½ teaspoon vanilla extract

1. To make the dough: In a small bowl, combine the flaxseed and water and stir to mix. Let sit at room temperature until thickened, about 5 minutes. Then transfer the flaxseed mixture to a medium bowl and stir in the milk, melted butter, and coffee.

2. In the bowl of a stand mixer fitted with the dough hook, combine the flour, sugar, yeast, salt, cinnamon, and nutmeg. Pour the liquid ingredients into the dry ingredients and mix on low speed until well combined, about 3 minutes. If the dough becomes too sticky, add flour, 1 tablespoon at a time, until it is slightly tacky to the touch.

3. On a lightly floured surface, form the dough into a ball and then place in a large lightly greased bowl. Cover loosely with a kitchen towel, and let rest for 10 to 15 minutes to relax the gluten.

4. To make the filling: In a small bowl, combine the brown sugar and cinnamon and stir to mix.

5. Transfer the dough to a lightly floured work surface and roll out to a 10 by 12-inch rectangle about ¼ inch thick. Spread the room-temperature butter evenly across the surface of the dough and sprinkle the cinnamon-sugar all over, leaving a ¼-inch margin.

6. With the long side facing you and using your hands, roll the dough into a tight cylinder, pinching to seal the seam. Using dental floss or a bread knife, cut the cylinder into ten to twelve equal pieces. (Dental floss allows for a cleaner cut and keeps the rolls intact, preserving their beautiful shape.) Lightly grease a 9-inch round cake pan or 9 by 13-inch baking pan. Place the cinnamon rolls 1-inch apart in the prepared pan.

7. Drizzle the warm coconut cream over the rolls, cover the pan with a kitchen towel, and set aside in a warm place until the rolls have doubled in size, about 1 hour.

8. Preheat the oven to 350°F. Bake the cinnamon rolls until golden brown, 20 to 25 minutes. If the tops are browning too quickly, cover loosely with aluminum foil and continue baking. Remove the cinnamon rolls from the pan and let cool on a wire rack for 10 to 15 minutes.

9. To make the maple butter: In a small bowl, combine the maple syrup, melted butter, and vanilla and stir to incorporate.

10. Serve the cinnamon rolls, warm, with the maple butter on the side to drizzle over or dip into.

WINTERGREEN
(GAULTHERIA PROCUMBENS)

Have you ever had Winterfresh gum? It was my dad's favorite, and the flavor is quite close to that of the wintergreen plant. Wintergreen is a low-growing evergreen that flowers and produces fruit. The entire plant is edible, and there are typically plenty of plants growing in one area. They are an easy foraging find because their red berries pop against snowy landscapes during the winter months. Additionally, the whole plant has a strong, minty aroma, which makes it easily identifiable. To find wintergreen, you'll have to watch your step in the woods. Carefully collect the whole plant in a plastic container with a lid to avoid smashing the delicate berries. With wintergreen, a little bit goes a long way when it comes to creating extractions or using it for cooking purposes.

Appearance: Low-growing plant. Leathery, oval, mildly toothed leaves 1 to 2 inches long. Typically three or four leaves present per plant; become tinged with red in chilly weather. In summer, dangly, bell-shaped white flowers with five lobes at tips. Small red berries are present from fall to spring.

Smell: Strong minty aroma.

Taste: Crisp, refreshing flavor.

Habitat: Full to partial shade in moist, acidic soils. Often found in woodlands filled with hemlock trees.

Region: Native to North America; commonly found in eastern and northeastern United States, including Maine, New Hampshire, Vermont, Massachusetts, Connecticut, New York, Pennsylvania, and throughout the Appalachian Mountains.

Growth Cycle: Grows a few inches each year in a creeping rhizomatic (horizontal underground stem growth) fashion.

Prime Harvest Season: Berries ripen late summer through fall. Plant can be collected throughout winter.

Dangerous Lookalikes: Mountain laurel, a shrub that grows in similar habitats, is a dangerous lookalike to wintergreen when it first sprouts. Poisonous to humans. If you are unsure, crush a leaf between your fingers to check for a minty aroma. If no aroma, do not consume.

You can often find wintergreen where blueberries grow in the wild—they tend to prefer similar soil profiles.

Wintergreen extract is easy to make and is deeply flavorful. It is the strongest peppermint flavor you can think of and goes a very long way in any recipe. This extract takes a few weeks to make and is used in the recipes that follow.

WINTERGREEN EXTRACT

MAKES ABOUT 1 CUP

Special equipment: Sterilized 8-ounce mason jar with lid (see page 15)

½ cup wintergreen leaves, berries, and stems

½ cup vodka or grain alcohol, or as needed

1. In the mason jar, combine the wintergreen leaves, berries, and stems and enough of the vodka to cover completely. Seal the jar and set aside in a cool, dark place for at least 4 weeks or up to 6 weeks.

2. Shake the bottle once a week and check the infusion for flavor every 2 weeks, until the extract reaches your desired level of mint flavor.

3. Strain the extract and return it to the bottle. Store, tightly sealed, at room temperature for up to 6 months.

Every good wintergreen recipe starts with wintergreen extract, which adds a great burst of flavor. This wintergreen gimlet makes for a refreshing, light, holiday-inspired drink, perfect for family gatherings or to finish off an intimate dinner for two!

WINTERGREEN GIMLET

1. In a small saucepan over medium heat, combine the sugar and water and bring to a simmer. Let simmer, stirring occasionally, until all the sugar dissolves. Remove from the heat and set this simple syrup aside until cool. (Measure out 1 ounce for the drinks and store the reminder in an airtight container in the refrigerator for up to 1 month.)

2. Fill a cocktail shaker with ice, add the 1 ounce simple syrup, gin, lime juice, and wintergreen extract. Shake well until the shaker is cold to the touch, about 30 seconds. Strain and pour evenly into two rocks or coupe glasses.

3. Top each gimlet with a splash of prosecco, and garnish with cranberries, wintergreen leaves, and the lime wheels.

MAKES 2 SERVINGS

1 cup pure cane sugar

1 cup water

Ice cubes for shaking

3 ounces gin or nonalcoholic gin (such as Ritual Zero Proof)

1½ ounces lime juice, plus 2 lime wheels

½ teaspoon Wintergreen Extract (page 249)

2 splashes prosecco or tonic water

Cranberries and wintergreen leaves for garnishing

WINTERGREEN PATTIES

These patties remind me of mint–chocolate chip ice cream and peppermint patties. The first time that I tried mint–chocolate chip ice cream was at Sweet Claude's, the local ice-cream shop in my hometown. Something about the classic rich, creamy dessert studded with dark chocolate and a minty burst of flavor just did it for me. I captured those flavors in this quick-and-easy dessert, which you can keep in your freezer for whenever you crave something ice cold and minty.

MAKES 12 TO 14 PATTIES

3 cups confectioners' sugar, or as needed, sifted

⅔ cup sweetened condensed oat milk or condensed dairy milk

2 tablespoons salted, plant-based butter (such as Country Crock avocado oil), dairy butter, or refined coconut oil, melted

1 teaspoon Wintergreen Extract (page 249)

2 cups dark chocolate chips

Sprinkles or melted white chocolate for garnishing (optional)

1. Line a baking sheet with parchment paper.

2. In a large bowl, combine the confectioners' sugar, condensed milk, melted butter, and wintergreen extract and stir until they form a large ball.

3. Dust a work surface with confectioners' sugar. Place the ball on the surface and knead gently, adding a little more confectioners' sugar as needed, to form a cohesive, pliable dough.

4. Take 1-tablespoon chunks of the dough and, using your hands, form small round patties, 1½ to 2 inches in diameter and about ⅓ inch thick. Place the patties on the prepared baking sheet, about 1 inch apart. Cover the patties with another sheet of parchment paper. Place the baking sheet in the freezer for 15 minutes.

5. Meanwhile, line a second baking sheet with parchment paper. Fill a small saucepan with a few inches of water and set over low heat. Place a heatproof bowl on top of the pan, ensuring the bottom of the bowl does not touch the water.

6. Put the chocolate chips into the bowl and let melt, stirring occasionally for even heat distribution. Once the chocolate has melted, remove from the heat. (Alternatively, place the chocolate in a microwave-safe bowl and microwave on medium or low power in 15- to 20-second intervals. After each interval, stir the chocolate to distribute and continue until it is fully melted.)

7. Dip each frozen patty into the chocolate so that it's completely covered, allowing excess chocolate to drip off. Place on the prepared baking sheet. Repeat until all the patties have been dipped. Add sprinkles over the top or drizzle with melted white chocolate, if desired. Return to the freezer to firm up, about 30 minutes.

8. Transfer the patties to an airtight container, separating each layer with wax paper to prevent sticking, and then store in a cool, dry place at room temperature for up to 1 week or in the freezer for 3 to 4 months.

RESOURCES FOR LEARNING & IDENTIFYING PLANTS & FUNGI

Learning how to identify plants and fungi is no easy feat, but it's crucial. It's quite easy to misidentify plants and fungi, and doing so can mean an unnecessary upset stomach at best or, at worst, getting poisoned and rushed to the hospital. My aim with this book has been to provide you with the tools to avoid that, helping you to become a successful forager and chef. The goal, after all, is to have fun and cook safely with the wild edibles you have found. Here are my favorite resources for learning and identifying plants and fungi, as well as foraging do's and don'ts.

BOOKS

While there are many great, thorough identification guide books, following are some of my personal favorites. These books have largely shaped me into the forager I am today and have stuck out to me on my journey. I highly recommend finding books that are specific to your region, as plants and fungi often vary based on location.

Identifying and Harvesting Edible and Medicinal Plants in Wild (and Not So Wild) Places by Steve Brill and Evelyn Dean

This book teaches you how to identify and prepare more than five hundred different plants for nutrition and health. It offers a wealth of knowledge for curious foragers both new and experienced, with detailed drawings to aid in identification. It's a fantastic field guide to have on hand!

Mushrooms of the Northeast: A Simple Guide to Common Mushrooms by Teresa Marrone and Walt Sturgeon

If you live in the northeastern United States, this guide is a great place to start. I bring it out in the field with me, as it's quite small. Everything is explained in a way that is easy to understand, with a wide variety of photos to help you properly identify mushrooms.

Northeast Foraging: 120 Wild and Flavorful Edibles from Beach Plums to Wineberries by Leda Meredith

This book is a great resource for learning how to identify plant species that grow abundantly in the Northeast. Leda takes her time to educate you on the proper ways to identify plants, as well as how to harvest them.

National Audubon Society Field Guide to North American Mushrooms by National Audubon Society

This is, hands down, my favorite book for mushroom identification. Although some of the terminology is complex, there isn't a more complete guide to mushroom identification. It provides detailed content for every single mushroom that has been discovered within the United States, making it a genuine treasure. Additionally, it includes information on spore printing, with small sketches to help you better identify fungi. If you are already comfortable in the world of mushrooms and don't own this book, I still recommend adding it to your collection and taking it with you into the field to help you identify species that are new to you.

The Forager's Harvest: A Guide to Identifying, Harvesting, and Preparing Edible Wild Plants by Samuel Thayer

I love this book because it is succinct, cohesive, and easily understandable. There are a lot of photos in the book to help you identify and become familiar with several parts of any given plant, making it one of the most comprehensive plant guides available.

APPS

I don't tend to recommend smartphone applications for identifying plants and fungi. Users might rely on them as a completely accurate guide for identifying a species, and this presents serious risks. Variations in lighting, camera quality, and technological errors can contribute to the way an app identifies—or misidentifies—a plant or mushroom species. My advice is to allow these applications to serve as general guides that help you out in the field. But don't use them as your identification bibles. I strongly urge you to take home any plant species or fungus you want to identify and consult a reputable book. And when identifying fungi, always complete a spore print before eating.

iNaturalist

This app is a highly regarded one used by scientists, foragers, and inquisitive plant lovers alike. The creators' mission is to build a global community of people who will help educate folks about nature and biodiversity. The application allows you to share your observations, discuss with others, and log your observations and location when identifying certain species.

PictureThis

This application attempts to assist you with identifying plants, and also provides detailed information about each plant, once identified.

PictureMushroom

This application attempts to assist you with identifying fungi, providing detailed information about each species, with photos. It teaches you which mushrooms are in season, what they smell like, and where to find them. Typically, it will give you three to five results in addition to its top match, which can help you narrow the possibilities for what you've found.

Google Maps

I'm sure you weren't expecting this, but Google Maps has quickly become one of my favorite tools for foraging. It allows you to save approximate locations in an organized list, so you can always return to a specific foraging spot for the next harvest. For example, there is a place in my woods where I collect maitake mushrooms. It's in a very specific location, which I saved on my phone. And Google Maps is able to take me there on foot. Pretty cool stuff!

ONLINE COMMUNITIES

Online communities are wonderful places to connect with experienced foragers and learn about native plants in your area. Obviously, you should always be cautious in how and where you meet anyone online, but I have made many lifelong friendships with foraging mentors who are far more experienced than I, and I cherish them. Online communities help foster collaborative learning.

Facebook Forums

Most states have a local foraging forum in which you can learn, meet up, and develop your skills with a group of people. Often, experienced foragers will lead public meetups. In my state, there is a local foraging club that brings you out in the woods to forage, sort, and cook what you've found. I've been a member of the Foraging of Southern New England group and Mushrooms of Connecticut group for years. These forums have been immensely important to my journey and have helped me to become a better, more confident forager. Members tend to share recipes, techniques for preservation, and more. It's a whole lot of fun!

Reddit

The subreddit r/foraging is a great online community for foragers to share their experiences, ask questions, share images and resources, and learn from others. It has a large and active community of foraging enthusiasts. The only downside is that the group is not micro-focused on any specific geographical location. The environment is supportive and welcoming to newcomers, which fosters learning and encourages participation.

ACKNOWLEDGMENTS

To my wonderful mother and father, who molded and shaped me into who I am and taught me the importance of hard work and pursuing your passions with every fiber of your being, no matter the odds. To my siblings—Dillian, Nikki, Leslie, Don, Mary, and Faith—who have been my pillars of strength, my best friends, my shoulders to cry on, and my constant cheerleaders. To the Ofgang family—you have shown me love and grace in ways that I had never known before. You have supported and encouraged me beyond measure, and I am so lucky. Levon Ofgang, my partner— thanks for accompanying me on every foraging adventure over the last few years. I love you.

To *Bon Appétit* magazine, for taking a chance on me. To my amazing photographer, Natalie Black; you and I did this—we made it! We evolved together and handled every challenge as a team. To my foraging community, which has helped me to grow and bloom into the person who was able to write a book on the topic—thank you.

To my mentors, Gerry Moerschell, Michele Solstiak, and Chris Major, you have entrusted me with a wealth of knowledge and all the best foraging secrets that nature has to offer. I am so grateful. To Dave Paton, the moments we shared were brief but extremely impactful. Thank you for showing me Fiddlehead Island; it's one of the most beautiful places on Earth.

To Amanda Martinelli, my great friend who created the stunning pieces of pottery seen throughout the pages of this book—I love our creative collaboration and you mean so much to me. To Shakira Nieves and Gabriella Reyes, for joining me on so many random foraging outings and helping me with nature photography—I'm so lucky to call you both true friends.

To the team at Ten Speed Press who helped me shape a mere seed of an idea and bring it to reality: Zoey Brandt and Emma Campion, I appreciate your creativity beyond measure, and your patience with me. Thank you for trusting me with so many aspects of this book and allowing me to be the artist that I am in every form. To Karen Connelly, for helping me to edit this book when my words ran on endlessly—you always keep me in check.

To Foraging of Southern New England folks, who contributed to the Foraging 101 section of this book, including Eric Vanorden, Nick Pirraglia, Monica Pancare, Spike Mikulski, Kevyn Fowler, Amelia Kellner, Christine Gagnon, Kate Geruntho Frank, Jack Gilbert, Bill Yule, Ashley Ann Stanley, Ally Webb, and beyond. You taught me that foraging is more than just the treasure hunt—it means community and connection, which is of the utmost importance to me. To my friends and folks who have supported me from day one and believed in my vision, you know who you are.

And last, but certainly not least, to Brian McGovern—I wish you could've seen how this book turned out. You pushed me creatively and inspired me to stick to being myself and continuing to do work that fuels me. I am so grateful for the friendship we had and the deep connection we shared through our love of nature; rest easy my friend. Thank you.

Chrissy Tracey is a first-generation Jamaican American vegan chef, artist, forager, YouTuber, and entrepreneur in the food and wellness space. She is the first vegan chef to be featured on *Bon Appétit*'s *Test Kitchen* YouTube series and has been featured in the magazine. Her recipes and work have been featured in *Epicurious*, *Sanctuary*, *VegNews*, and the *Vegan Review*. She has also been showcased on the *Bon Appétit Food People* podcast and NPR's *Seasoned*. Tracey was listed in *Connecticut Magazine*'s 40 Under 40 and made a name for herself while working as a vegan pizza chef in New Haven, a city known all over the world for its pizza. She currently runs a Connecticut-based catering company, Eatwithchrissy, that specializes in curating unique plant-based culinary events.

Natalie Black is a photographer and digital media professional. She has provided brand work for clients including 20th Century Fox, Fandango, and the CW. She also led the visual creative direction and digital media footprint implementation for the Michelin star restaurants Crown Shy and SAGA, along with the World's 50 Best Bars #34, Overstory. She currently works as a freelance photographer and videographer for restaurants, chefs, and food brands around New York City. Her work has been featured in the *New York Times*, *Eater*, *New York Magazine*, *Michelin Guide*, *50 Best*, *New Yorker*, *Grub Street*, *Vogue*, *Time Out*, and *Today*.

INDEX

Note: Page references in *italics* indicate photographs.

Published in the United States by Ten Speed Press, an imprint of Random House, a division of Penguin Random House LLC, New York.
TenSpeed.com
RandomHouseBooks.com

Ten Speed Press and the Ten Speed Press colophon are registered trademarks of Penguin Random House LLC.

Additional photo credits:
Levon Ofgang, magnolia landscape, pages 20–21
Tyler Russell, Connecticut Public Radio, fiddlehead ID, page 58
Atlantic Sea Farms, kelp ID, pages 78–79
Lisa Nichols, Katsu Chicken of the Woods, page 126
Shakira Nieves, beach plum ID, page 133
Kathleen Capen, lion's mane ID, page 203

Typeface: FontFont Type's Mark Pro

Library of Congress Cataloging-in-Publication Data
Names: Tracey, Chrissy, 1994- author.
Title: Forage & feast : recipes for bringing mushrooms & wild plants to
  your table / by Chrissy Tracey.
Other titles: Forage and feast
Identifiers: LCCN 2023016960 (print) | LCCN 2023016961 (ebook) | ISBN
  9781984862242 (hardcover) | ISBN 9781984862259 (ebook)
Subjects: LCSH: Vegan cooking. | Cooking (Wild foods) | Wild plants,
  Edible. | Edible mushrooms. | LCGFT: Cookbooks.
Classification: LCC TX837 .T724 2024 (print) | LCC TX837 (ebook) | DDC
  641.5/6362—dc23/eng/20230417
LC record available at https://lccn.loc.gov/2023016960
LC ebook record available at https://lccn.loc.gov/2023016961

Hardcover ISBN: 978-1-9848-6224-2
eBook ISBN: 978-1-9848-6225-9

Printed in China

Editor: Zoey Brandt | Production editors: Doug Ogan and Natalie Blachere
Designer: Emma Campion | Production designers: Mari Gill and Faith Hague
Production manager: Dan Myers | Prepress color manager: Jane Chinn
Copyeditor: Deborah Kops | Proofreader: Rachel Holzman | Indexer: Ken DellaPenta
Publicist: Natalie Yera | Marketer: Monica Stanton

10 9 8 7 6 5 4 3 2 1

First Edition